Marni

Marni Bates

WITHDRAWN

HCI TEENS

Health Communications, Inc.
Deerfield Beach, Florida

www.hcibooks.com

This book is dedicated to
Frank and Dena Bates:
the former for pulling all the strings in heaven
and the latter for all the love and support on earth.
I would also like to thank my fellow hoosfooses
who made me the person I am today.
There would've been nothing to write without you.

Library of Congress Cataloging-in-Publication Data

Bates, Marni.
    Marni / Marni Bates.
        p. cm.
    ISBN-13: 978-0-7573-1412-4
    ISBN-10: 0-7573-1412-0
    1. Family.   I. Title.
    HQ503.B38 2009
    306.85—dc22

                                                            2009017813

Publisher: Health Communications, Inc.
            3201 S.W. 15th Street
            Deerfield Beach, FL 33442–8190

Cover photo © Simon Dearden/Corbis
Cover design by Larissa Hise Henoch
Interior design and formatting by Lawna Patterson Oldfield

Introduction

WHEN I TOLD MY SIBLINGS I was writing an autobi-
ography at the tender age of nineteen, their laughter blared
over the telephone straight into my ear. The general consen-
sus was that I hadn't done enough, experienced enough, to be
worthy of the ink. And at first, I agreed with them. In fact,
it wasn't until I flipped through my old journals that I realized why I agreed to this endeavor. Buried somewhere in
between angst-ridden sentences was a girl with real problems who deserved to be heard. So here it is: my tale of tri-
als and tribulations, awkwardness and awesomeness. My
story isn't about when bad things happen to good people. It's
about how people grow, adapt, bond, and break apart. More
specifically, it's about how I became the person I am today.
If I had a better sense of who that is, this book would have
been much easier to write. Instead, I'll try to leave judgment
to you, the reader. Whether I am a freak, an inspiration, a
nut case, a survivor, a mess, or a combination of all of the
above is for you to decide. All I know for certain is that I am
Marni Bates, and this is where my story begins.

Chapter I

I HAVE A TON OF IRRATIONAL FEARS. I refuse to cross streets without a clear sign that it is my turn to walk. I am afraid of driving because I have trouble telling my left from my right. I am scared of snakes, spiders, beef jerky, unnaturally-colored foods (like Jell-O), and technology in its many forms. I also fear spandex. Don't ask me why. What I try really hard not to fear is the truth. I always want to know who should be held responsible, even if it's me. And a lot of the time, it is me. Sometimes I don't even realize that until years later, when I wake up and think, *Wow, how lame am I for trying to blame someone else for that?* Answer: exceedingly lame.

So I don't blame anyone else for my hair pulling. I refuse to bore you by wailing about how if it hadn't been for my dad, or my sister, or our beauty-obsessed consumerist society, my life would have turned out differently. Partly, because it just isn't true. All of those were factors (maybe even large factors), but they don't explain why I have an insistent craving to reach up and pull out my hair. Why I long for the rip and relish the sensation. And I suspect that blaming my love of pulling on other people is just as fruitless as blaming Toll House for my love of raw cookie dough. There are times when people need to stiffen their spine, nod their head, and admit they do it to themselves. For me, that's pulling.

It didn't start out as this big convoluted heap of ugliness in my life. It turned into that, sure, but at the beginning it was something much purer. I wasn't doing it to be mean to myself, or to punish myself, or to abuse myself. It wasn't nearly so dramatic or masochistic. I honestly thought I was beautifying myself. A little part of me even thought that pulling might make my life better. Maybe if my eyebrows were more attractive, people would notice me as being someone special. Maybe then I wouldn't feel like I was always being passed over and slotted in the role of the understudy sidekick who would only be in the play if something happened to someone else. I honestly thought that if I were prettier (and had the self-confidence that goes with it), maybe my life would be better. I thought pulling my eyebrows was one way to get there. It didn't work out that way.

Instead, I found myself clutching long strands of hair I had ripped from my head, unable to stop myself from reaching up and wanting more. My pulling was never supposed to take on a life of its own—it was never supposed to take over mine. I knew it had, though. When I stared at the mirror and tried to recognize the girl without eyebrows, eyelashes, and bangs as myself and failed, I knew something had gone horribly wrong. It's hard to recognize yourself when you've pulled at your eyebrows so consistently that there is almost nothing left. It's hard to believe you could have done something so destructive to your face, and that tomorrow you have to go to school pretending nothing is different.

At some point in my life, I stopped being Marni and instead turned into an addict who ravaged her head when she didn't think anyone was looking. I pulled during breakfast, lunch, and dinner. I pulled at school, in restaurants, in grocery lines, in my room, in the bathroom. If I were in a Dr. Seuss book, I would pull in a box, I would pull with a fox, I would pull here and there, I would pull most everywhere. There was no way to escape it. Hair has a tendency to travel with a person—it's even more persistent than a shadow that way—and mine came with an incredible temptation to zone out and lose myself in the soothing rhythm of my plucking.

How did I get this way? I still wonder that sometimes. How is it possible that I am so consumed, so obsessed, with something that brings no real comfort to me? Why can't I stop? Why must I make a New Year's resolution to kick the habit, only to end up hating myself even more when I am at it again the next day? Why am I so ashamed of something I don't feel I have control over? How did I go from a happy-go-lucky kindergartener who believed in fairies, to a teenager with the urge to yank, pinch, and pull until there is nothing left to grab? Some of these answers I just don't have. To be honest, I don't know if anyone has them. How did I get here, though? Well, that I should be able to tell you. All we have to do is go back to my childhood and my very first lie.

Chapter 2

I CAN'T REMEMBER A TIME when I couldn't read. I took to it so naturally that I never needed an adult to help me sound out the words. Assistance of any kind was quickly deemed completely unnecessary. The librarians readily handed over the more advanced books and wracked their heads for a series that would engross me long enough until they came up with something else. I happily spent the majority of my childhood curled up on the nearest couch, lost to my surroundings. In elementary school, I read during lunch, through recess, while walking home, after school, and before bed. My best friend, Gwyn, would shake her head with a mixture of amusement and disgust when I'd nearly walk into parked cars and trees because I was focusing solely on a book. Gwyn let everyone know I was one strange kid, which didn't exactly come as a shock—they knew it already.

Not that I was some prodigy who only found comfort in the complete works of Shakespeare. If someone made me pick between a book and an ice cream cone, I would be biting into the crispy crust before the question was finished. In many respects, I was painfully normal. I had a normal fear of phys ed class (especially anything that involved tumbling, running, rolling, climbing, jumping, or coordination of any kind) and a strong sense of self-preservation. I didn't read everywhere to prove I was special or different. I did it because, even at the age of five, I knew I wanted nothing to do with reality. It was *way* too messy.

In the imaginary world I refused to leave, I wasn't the runt of the family, pushed around by my older siblings Jordan, Jonathan, and Shayna. I didn't have to listen to the constant bickering and fighting that comes with sibling rivalry. My own mother never cried in any of the stories I read. My world was contained in a bubble full of mystery and freedom. I couldn't understand why anyone would want to join "reality" when they could have amazing adventures with King Arthur and Merlin. So, I would grab a book, peer inside, and escape. It soon became the easiest, most natural thing in the world.

Reading was by no means my only method of evasion. I also used GRS (Golden Retriever System) to romp fearlessly around the neighborhood with our family dog, Rusty. Since Rusty always found his way home, I had more faith in him than a map or a compass. I reasoned that if I stuck by his side, nothing bad could happen. Together, we frolicked all over the neighborhood, returning to find the police and a frantic mother waiting for us. All the warnings in the world wouldn't have made much of an impression on me.

No matter what anyone said, acorn caps were really fairy boats and trees were really magical giants who guarded me while I slept. Mythical beings and magic were barely out of my reach, and I was certain that if it hadn't been for my birthday, I would have been happily whiling the days away with the fairies. My birthday was the one thing I knew had gone horribly wrong.

I should have been born on Halloween. All the rules of magic and nature agreed *that* should have been the day. Instead, due to an incompetent doctor who showed up several hours late, I entered the world in the wee small hours of the morning on November 1st. I blamed my lack of magical powers entirely on this birthing misfortune. The Disney Channel movie *Halloweentown* didn't help improve my spirits. The main character, Marnie, was born on Halloween, and she could cast spells and visit a magical world where Halloween never ended. Our almost identical names and birthdays were undeniable similarities and informed me of the truth: my birthday was a mistake that a magical being (aka my elusive fairy godmother) needed to remedy. She never showed up though, and I learned rather bitterly that fairies weren't to be depended upon. If my special powers had arrived, I would have consoled myself by reflecting that being born on the Day of the Dead was still interesting. Since they didn't, however, and I was likewise cursed with muddy brown hair, equally dark eyes (which my brother Jonathan kindly described as dog-poop brown), and a well-padded stomach, I refused to be soothed.

Just because my magic powers didn't show up didn't stop me from reading about them. I soaked in everything I could find on heroines and heroes, dwelling in particular on King Arthur. I loved that the scrawny underdog pulled out the sword and emerged triumphant. Happily ever afters in any story made me feel euphoric. I felt so strongly for the characters I would cheer and moan and rejoice for them. Sometimes, I would sit happily under a bush listening to a book on tape and wonder whether life would work out perfectly for me. I also wanted to know if I could train a bird to carry messages to Gwyn. To be honest, I still have no idea. Not about the bird—that question was firmly negated.

Reading became my life, and my life became reading. It

was also the subject of my first lie. Long before I turned five, I had convinced my dad that I didn't know how to read. This wasn't exactly a difficult feat to accomplish. My father's life was based in his accounting firm in Los Angeles; mine, in a messy room in Ashland, Oregon. Given that my parents' marriage was still intact at the time, this living arrangement might appear strange. Whether or not it was conventional, it was still highly agreeable to everyone. My father could work without giving his family a second thought and visit when it was convenient, while my mom could raise her four children with little interference. The only reason my parents were able to stay married for so long was because they didn't share a house (or even a state). This arrangement also made it pathetically easy to convince my dad of my illiteracy.

Looking back, I can make a pretty good guess as to why I pretended I couldn't read. It wasn't because I didn't want my dad to think of me as intelligent. I wanted him to be impressed with me. I wanted him to love me. I lied because I knew that intellect wasn't the way to his heart. After all, he didn't like my sister Shayna, and she read voraciously as well. Since he wasn't impressed with that, I thought maybe illiteracy would do the trick. I didn't realize at the time it was a desperate ploy for attention. My four-year-old self couldn't grasp what was going on. What I could understand was its immediate success. All I had to do was feign ignorance around my dad, and I was in. So, I stuttered and bumbled through picture books I could have read upside down with one eye closed and felt rewarded with his attention. My dad had no idea I was acting, which is no compliment to his intelligence as I have always been a lousy liar. He just didn't know me well enough to tell. My plan worked; I became Daddy's little girl. He chose me to be his favorite child. And for a while, that was all I could ever imagine wanting.

Chapter 3

THE DIVORCE DIDN'T COME as a surprise, as the marriage had always been more fiction than fact. When my dad did come home to visit, the quality of life deteriorated for everyone. He spent the majority of the time on the telephone making angry business calls. The rest of his time was spent pressuring Jordan, dismissing Jonathan, reprimanding Shayna, and doting upon me. I have to admit that back then, from where I was standing, things could have been considerably worse. I could do no wrong; Shayna, no right. I think my dad sensed from the beginning that Shayna possessed a strength of will and conviction that I lacked. He was looking for someone who was easy to manipulate, and there was no one with less resistance than me.

In the movies, being the favorite child always comes with benefits like bigger weekly allowances or later curfews. For me, there weren't any perks except the assurance that Daddy liked me. We didn't really do anything meaningful together in Ashland. My dad never quite understood the concept of "special time"—ultimately it was all about him. If I suggested we go see a movie, I would find myself watching an artsy Nepalese film about Sherpas. The film made up with subtitles what it lacked in plot. Not so much fun when you are seven years old.

My most treasured moments with him were fairly indistinguishable from his work. The proud owner of the local Laundromat, my dad would take us down to the store every time he came to town. We were then granted the privilege of entering dark, lonesome, tunnel-like rooms behind the rows of machines. That was where the real excitement hummed; it was a miniworld composed exclusively of cement, canals, and soaking treasures. The machines thoughtfully dumped money left carelessly in pockets into the waterways before me. I spent hours in the detergent-scented tunnels searching for a prize, lost in mystery and darkness. It was an alien place unlike any other, and I loved it. It never occurred to me to be upset my dad was always busy arguing with one of the managers and ignoring all of us. As much as I enjoyed going to the

Laundromat, it wasn't enough to make me wish he visited more frequently. Most of the time, I wanted him gone just like everyone else. The house never felt right when he was in it.

So, when my parents led me into their bedroom and explained that the marriage was over, I didn't really care. I don't think I really understood what it meant. Sure, I knew the concept of divorce: two people no longer together. What I couldn't see was what difference that would mean for me. Nothing seemed to change in the slightest. My mom still loved me, and my dad still visited when it suited him. The only real contrast was that instead of visiting the Laundromat, he was dragging my mom through an ugly divorce. My mom did her best to hide this from me. She didn't want any of us to feel stuck in the middle. In my case, she was entirely successful because I felt no urge to pry deeper. Divorce didn't belong in my imaginary world, and I had no intention of incorporating it.

My nonchalance about the whole thing concerned many parents at my elementary school. Polite, perpetually upbeat, and charmingly innocent, I was an easy kid for people to worry about. Mothers in particular hated the idea that I was being ripped apart by the strain of divorce. They would approach me, eyebrows furrowed in unease, and ask deep, probing questions.

"Are you all right?"

"How are you hanging in there?"

"And how does that make you feel?"

They never expected my answers.

"Everything is great. I feel fine. He visits all the time. Never been better. We're all okay. Really. Thanks for asking."

I honestly thought I was telling the truth. As far as I was concerned, everything continued without a hitch. In fact, things only got better, because at that point, I had also discovered the first Harry Potter book. I felt an instant connection with the "Boy Who Lived." We were both spending our formative years surrounded by Muggles who couldn't understand that we were just plain different. My mom had read the first one aloud to us before it was popular, and I was instantly hooked. By the time my elementary teacher agreed to read it to the class, I had it memorized. I mouthed all the words in perfect time, not caring that my classmates were staring at me instead of the teacher.

Immersed in the world of Harry Potter, I was sheltered from the divorce. When my spirits dragged, I concentrated on writing a sequel to the first Harry Potter book, divining things in my crystal ball, using a quill and ink, and building a hammock outside my room. All that I was able to create was a few sloppy pages of writing (my one attempt at fan fiction) and a large blue stain on my carpet where the ink spilled. Still, I was diverted from the battle that was raging around me. I didn't have to worry about any of the big questions: *Who gets the kitchen table? The cabinets? The kids?*

I was oblivious but not stupid. Eventually, I noticed the change. It wasn't hard to figure out once my dad stopped visiting. He disappeared from Ashland and only set foot in the town a handful of times once the divorce was finalized. Years later, he told me it was because it was "too hard . . . emotionally." I don't believe a word of it, especially since it took him so long to come up with that excuse. In the beginning, he just demanded we fly down to see him.

Since all of my relatives, from my grandparents to my cousins, lived in Los Angeles, flying to see him wasn't that unreasonable of a request. In fact, it worked out pretty well for everyone. We usually spent the first night at my grandparents' house before Dad would collect my siblings and me. My mom stayed with her parents until we were ready to go home.

The best parts of those trips were the times I spent with my grandparents. We'd watch old movies, do the morning word jumble, feed the squirrels, and tell stories together. Their house was on the short list of my favorite places in the whole wide world. It was neat and clean without feeling sterile. Better yet, it was filled with decidedly unusual purchases from their travels. Colorful rugs entertained me for hours, and I carefully traced patterns in them with my feet. More than the objects, I loved the people inside the house and the relatives who visited.

Visiting my dad wasn't the highlight of those visits. I felt obliged to spend time with him, but I doubt I felt real happiness. Seeing him was sort of like applying for a job. I paid so much attention to being on my best behavior (all smiles and enthusiasm) that I couldn't really relax. My grandparents didn't require that type of effort. I could be me. Once I left the safety of their house, however, that wasn't the case anymore.

I don't know why he wanted us to come in the first place. In the movies, the dad always misses the children horribly and does anything to see them. My dad didn't belong on the Disney Channel. If he missed us, he sure had an odd way of showing it. As soon as we got to his home, we were piled into his car and then dropped off to see his mother, our Grandma Joyce. The only time we actually spent with Dad was limited to the car rides back and forth and an occasional museum outing. Even when we were in the same city, I hardly saw him. So much for bonding.

He came up with a way to explain the situation: it was my mom's fault. If she just allowed him more time, then he could spend a few days with us after our stay with Grandma Joyce. Of course, if he hadn't dumped us at her house, he could have done that anyway. My dad didn't see the logic behind that simple idea.

What he did see was the opportunity to create a convenient system for himself. He thought he fulfilled his paternal responsibilities by picking us up, dropping us off, and going back to work. Blaming the arrangement on my mom was just icing on the cake. If anyone asked how we were doing, he could shake his head mournfully and say that he hadn't seen us lately because of the divorce. Meanwhile, at Grandma Joyce's house, the four of us were waiting to go home.

Her house was the complete opposite of my other grandparents' home; it was an unmitigated disaster, with gargantuan piles of junk everywhere. The only area where a clumsy girl could walk without fear of tripping was in the garden. That was where my siblings and I were soon put to work. No visit was complete until we had done our share of manual labor. We had a complicit understanding that boiled down to "You scratch my back, and I'll scratch yours." In this case it was "You pick up disgusting rotten fruit, and I'll take you to a museum." All things considered, this was not a bad deal. Sometimes it came with smoothies and *Doctor Dolittle*. Most of the time though, our reward was listening to her complain.

Everyone has different talents, and Grandma Joyce has a natural gift at whining. If she was forced not to complain, I suspect she would become a mute. Very little was agreeable in her eyes. Things she approved of were limited to:

1. Her son

2. Her garden

3. Discounts

And for a while, she approved of me. Probably for the same reason my dad did—because I was eager to be loved and easy to control.

Her favorite topics to moan about were my mom, the divorce, and Shayna. This didn't change even when Shayna was in the room. In fact, that was when Grandma Joyce encouraged me to tell Shayna what I really thought of her. Grandma Joyce even made me practice ordering an imaginary Shayna to back off and leave me alone. Since Shayna hated me and tried to walk all over me, I can understand why Grandma Joyce thought I needed protection. Unfortunately, she was just making a bad situation far worse.

Shayna had plenty of provocation to hate me. My spineless, bobble-headed submissiveness to Grandma Joyce was just another complaint to add to the list; it wasn't the real reason for her enmity—that had begun long before Grandma Joyce ever contributed to the problem. As soon as Dad decided to love me over her, I had become the enemy. As far as she was concerned, I was the devil in sister's clothing.

Dad's preference was too marked to be a matter of opinion. It was a fact. I was his favorite child and had been since before I could even walk. It wasn't a position I competed for, but one I heartily accepted. I loved being loved. Shayna hated being hated. It's not hard to guess which one of us got the short end of the stick. Dad and Grandma Joyce had trouble even tolerating her.

After stewing over what happened for years, I think I understand how it all fell apart. Once my dad realized Shayna could not be manipulated, he cast her aside. She in turn cast me aside. This left me at the mercy of my father when abroad and at the mercy of her when at home. Shayna's contempt for me only became more pronounced over time. She hated me with an intensity she didn't even try to conceal. We fought over everything and nothing.

I desperately wanted Shayna to love me, so I hatched a plan. I thought if we could bond over something, she would learn to like me. It seemed like a sensible idea, so I waited for an opening.

Everyone believed Shayna was the writer in the family. She fit the bill perfectly, especially considering the notebooks she perpetually carried around. Our family predicted Shayna was an Emily Dickinson in the works. Without having read so much as a page, I was positive her writing was brilliant. Shayna had a way of speaking that with each syllable proved her intellectual superiority. I couldn't imagine her writing would be any less intense, and I bowed before her acerbic tongue and sharp wit. Secure in my inferiority, I decided to write something of my own so we could bond over writing. Everyone loved it. Everyone except Shayna, that is. According to her, it was a shameless imitation of one of her stories I had overheard. What's worse, she saw it as an artless, calculating ploy to get attention.

My protests and apologies were flatly ignored. What I had intended to bring us together only drove us further apart. Shayna banned me from reading her favorite books and swore that never again could I read her writing, since I would just try to copy it. Her rants about plagiarism cemented in my mind, and I began to fear writing. I was afraid that maybe she was right about all of it.

So I took a lesson from the ostriches and hid my head in the sand (or in my case, books) until the danger was averted. Like the ostriches, I soon learned my approach wasn't the most effective way to handle problems. There was no way to escape my family life, be it my dad or my sister. The divorce made neutrality an illusion and impartiality a farce. I had to pick a side. The question was . . . *whose?*

Chapter 4

MY REALIZATION THAT I HAD no real relationship with my dad came about through a series of small epiphanies. I began to notice things I had missed before. Slowly, I discovered ulterior motives everywhere I looked.

When he didn't dump me with Grandma Joyce, my dad either took me to his office or to museums. Of course, I preferred the museums (with the notable exception of a Holocaust exhibit that haunted me for months) since there was always something to look at. His office, on the other hand, afforded no entertainment. I was so bored, I actually gave his assistant free back massages. At the time, I would have paid her for helping, ever so slightly, to relieve the interminable dullness.

Then there were the few solo trips I took to see him. Instead of curling up next to a fire with hot chocolate for some good old-fashioned bonding, we went to parties. Not fun parties. Nope. Bar and bat mitzvah parties of distant and unknown relatives, because nothing says togetherness like a roomful of strangers. In many ways, I was arm candy. Or arm bubblegum to be more precise. Dad picked me up in my brand-new velvet dress and then set to work parading me around. He saw me as a way to make himself look better. More impressive. He wasn't just an accountant if I was around. Suddenly, he had the title of "father" as well. I was just tossed around in his quest for admiration. "This is *my* daughter," he'd proclaim obnoxiously, "Isn't she great? It's such a pity about the divorce. I miss her terribly." All of these dramatics were performed while I was studiously ignored. The events felt so contrived and fake that I wanted to rip up my dress and curl into a ball. Instead, I was serenaded by "Baby Got Back." Listening to a song devoted to the wonders of big butts at a stranger's bar or bat mitzvah with my dad was too uncomfortable for words.

Nevertheless, I discounted my feelings of insecurity and kept suppressing myself around him. I thought the parties would make him love me more. I hoped that, somehow, my dad would care about me the same way my friend Gwyn's dad loved her: unconditionally and wholeheartedly. It didn't happen.

Slowly, painfully, I realized my dad and I would never have that sort of connection. This became a fact, not merely an unwanted thought, during what I dubbed the Vacation of the Music Man. It was to be an experience of a lifetime. My dad invited me, and only me, to be his companion on a trip to Costa Rica. I was thrilled to go, and the timing seemed impeccable. I was about to enter middle school, which meant that I was ready for anything. I imagined it as a spectacular adventure (which only proves, once again, that I never got the magical power of predicting the future).

The plan was simple. I would spend a week with him in Los Angeles (without Grandma Joyce for a change) before we left the country. Once we returned, I'd go back to my mom's. I thought the week in Los Angeles would be more than long enough to fulfill my daydreams of long conversations and good-natured laughter. I envisioned the two of us playing cards for hours.

Instead, he merely substituted Grandma Joyce with his girlfriend. He dumped me at her house and, with a pat on the head, went to work. Andrea, who I never heard of until we were introduced, was a kind and attractive woman. A single mother with two sons, she was also a lawyer who looked more than capable of handling herself in court. Her smile was warm, but a rather cross default expression made me fear she was secretly displeased with me. We did have one thing in common though: we both deserved far better than my father.

Andrea and her boys were perfectly wonderful to me. It wasn't their fault I was miserable. The only serious flaw I found in Andrea was that she didn't confront my dad about leaving his daughter alone in a strange house for a week. To be fair, I suppose that might not be the best thing to do when you are trying to keep a boyfriend.

I became the California version of fictional recluse Boo Radley and morphed into a complete shut-in. I didn't know the neighborhood, so I couldn't leave the house. I didn't want to risk losing my way and having no one to find me. Since I couldn't escape the house, I did my very best to disappear. I hadn't packed sufficient reading material and was thus reduced to watching *Free Willy* and *The Music Man* multiple times each day. In between screenings and chocolate chip cookies (which served as my breakfast, lunch, and snack), I read *FoxTrot* comic strips. Up until then, my experience with cartoons had been limited to *Garfield,* and my introduction to *FoxTrot* couldn't have come at a better time. I sprawled out on the floor in the boys' room and read comics until they began to blur.

I realize that in many ways my vacation sounds great. Comic strips? Check. Movies? Check. Massive amounts of sugar? Check. I should have been happy. That's what I kept telling myself anyway. *I should be happy right now.* The thought helped me slap on a brave face and pretend to be cheerful. Once again, my dad didn't see past my truly awful acting. I guess he didn't care enough to look deeper, which just made me miss my mom dreadfully. She could tell something was up just by the strain in my voice over the phone. I even missed my dad—not my actual father so much as the fantasy of him I constructed. I wanted that back. The mythical world I had created wasn't as protective anymore. Reality was creeping in.

In many ways, Costa Rica was even worse. The flight in particular stands out, thanks to all its awkward glory. My dad had complained his way into getting us adjacent seats in first class, which would have been exciting if it weren't for the fact that he had nothing to say to me. After being in a state of solitary isolation at Andrea's, what I wanted most was a little human interaction. I got zilch. *Nada.* Nothing. So, we just sat next to each other in silence and waited for the in-flight entertainment.

If I had known that *Edtv* was the movie, I might have refused to board the plane. Okay, I'm exaggerating. I just would have made arrangements to parachute off the damn thing when my dad began slobbering over a half-naked woman who filled up the screen. His greasy hair only helped illuminate his expression as things got increasingly . . . intimate. I was repulsed. Absolutely grossed out. Even today, the memory makes me wrinkle my nose and grimace. At the time, I just hoped things would improve once my feet were on the ground. Frankly, not a whole lot changed.

Sure, we were in Costa Rica, but we *still* had nothing to say. Maybe part of the problem was that my dad saw me as the innocent bobblehead he taught to read: Daddy's little girl. But, I didn't feel like that girl anymore. Reality had intruded, and now I noticed things like a lack of birthday presents, telephone calls, and visits. He'd say he missed me, but he never tried to change things. He didn't even know how to hug me. I wanted a real relationship, and he didn't know what that meant. Maintaining the appearance of the good, All-American Dad was the only thing he understood. The silence between us was deafening, so I tried to stimulate conversation. The only foolproof topic I could think of was the divorce—I knew he could talk about that forever. The price I had to pay for conversation was listening to him insult my mom. What confused me most was that I hated talking about the divorce, yet, I was the one instigating it. This left me with a very important question: *what the hell was I doing to myself?*

I had no answer and returned home thoroughly confused. My dad and I were still strangers. Somehow, our trip to Costa Rica hadn't been enough. Staring into lush forests, horseback riding up a volcano, flying through trees on zip lines . . . none of it had been enough. We still had nothing to say. What I didn't know was that all too soon I would have plenty to say—and none of it good.

Chapter 5

I HAVE NEVER UNDERSTOOD BOYS. Or men. The male species in general. My dad is an excellent example, as he made absolutely no sense to me when I was growing up. He'd say one thing and do something completely different. I couldn't just pretend it was opposite day, either. It wasn't that up was down with him. Instead up was actually down, reversed, and to the left. Confused? So was I. In fact, there were only a handful of truths I knew for sure:

1. I didn't want to give up on our relationship.

2. We had almost nothing by way of a relationship.

3. I couldn't stand to hear him criticize my mom.

This last truth was probably the most important. My mom had always been the very best thing in my life. Growing up, one of the reasons I craved my dad's affection was because my mom's was never denied. The two of us had a habit of cuddling on rainy days and playing the "I love you more than . . ." game.

"I love you more than all the socks in all the world," I'd tell her as I snuggled deeper into her side.

She would stroke my hair comfortingly. "I love you more than all the stars in the sky."

"More than all the socks and shoes," I'd proclaimed earnestly.

"More than all the grains of sand."

I never had to wonder if she really meant it, either, which was why seeing my dad tore me up inside. He vilified her, blaming the divorce, our infrequent visits . . . everything on my mom. He verbally cut down the woman who had single-handedly raised me. And I would listen, grin, and bear it.

My mom, on the other hand, never said a word. She never criticized my dad, and she never discussed the divorce with me. Trashing my dad would have hurt us, and she wasn't willing to have her ranting come at the price of our happiness. Her primary concern was keeping the four of us emotionally safe. She did everything she could to ensure our preserved peace of mind, including going to therapy.

I think she would have gotten a whole lot more out of her sessions if it hadn't been for Richard. After the divorce, my mom reunited with her ex-boyfriend, and soon there was yet another male in my life (and house) who I didn't understand. While my mom didn't regret marrying or divorcing my dad (she said her four children were worth every minute of it), she certainly regretted Richard. He was the biggest male mistake of her life. He was one ex who should have remained an ex.

Richard was an "artist" and just as moody as the term vaguely implies. He believed the definition of a true artist was one who suffers greatly. In order to fit this description, he took to haunting the house in a foul mood. Whenever he couldn't sleep, he stationed himself in the living room, glowering fiercely at the television through the night. Richard prided himself on feeling everything intensely. Accordingly, when he wasn't happy, everyone knew about it. His mood swings scared me. He pretended they were normal and proudly discussed his time in therapy. He thought it was amazing that he'd been transformed from a mess into a true artist. I doubt the transformation (if any had even occurred) really stuck.

Long story short, my mom wasn't happy, my sister wasn't friendly, my oldest brother Jordan left home early (because of

Richard), and my other brother Jonathan spent all his time locked up in his room. I lived in a house full of people who weren't really there. It was a lonely world and I was armed with just my books to ward off depression.

In the middle of this mess was my dad. He just sort of molded in California while things got increasingly worse in Oregon. He didn't call, and we didn't talk—not because I objected to it, but because there was nothing to say. I didn't stop visiting him, but my trips became less frequent. They were limited to bat and bar mitzvah parties. I guess having an escort was losing some of the appeal. I didn't enjoy the trips but still looked forward to the possibility of connection with my dad they offered. I continued to hope that someday we would have the real father-daughter experience.

Eventually, however, I just couldn't believe anymore.

Things changed during my first solo trip to Los Angeles. I'd become accustomed to traveling with someone older and wiser and felt very important flying as an unaccompanied minor. I was also terrified of the Los Angeles International Airport. Everyone was wheeling luggage and rushing off to unknown destinations while I stood outside the terminal utterly confused. I didn't know who to follow. I had no idea what I was supposed to be doing. Several hours later, my dad collected me from airport personnel, and I felt like a princess who had just been rescued. I also felt a little cranky that it had taken him so long to do it. Still, I was relieved to be under my dad's watch. For a little while, anyway.

This trip included another infamous bar mitzvah dog and pony show. "Baby Got Back" still wasn't comfortable—no matter how many times I had heard it around my dad, it was to remain perpetually awkward. Actually, everything about the parties felt awkward to me. My dad always urged me to join in the dance where the family was supposed to circle the person being celebrated, so I would end up doing the grapevine around a complete stranger (second cousin once removed or some such thing), feeling completely out of place. The celebrations were always over-the-top, with glass-blowing stalls and other extravagant projects I couldn't imagine people affording.

This particular event was memorably lousy. For the first time, someone (I believe one of my unknown cousins) was being friendly. He gave me a sailor's cap, we danced around, and, for a brief second, I had fun. For some reason, this made me want to cry, and I fought back tears all the way to my dad's apartment. I probably sound ridiculous. I enjoyed a party and therefore wanted to bawl like a three-year-old. I think it was mainly because I didn't expect it. I was so used to being ignored and awkward that inclusion felt odd. The worst part was that it had been fantastic, and I doubted it would happen again. My dad never noticed any change in my mood.

My visits in California were always brief. I guess my dad didn't need an escort after the event was over. The whole thing felt devised to be as impersonal as possible. I went to a party, saw a museum, and flew home. On this trip, my dad took me to the library the same day I was scheduled to leave Los Angeles. *Why*, I wondered silently, *is he doing this? Does he want to spend as little time with me as possible? Surely that's crazy though, right?*

The weather matched my mood. Sunny California had been replaced with bitterly cold wind, thick fog, and sopping wet streets. Winter had set in with a vengeance and had no intention of relinquishing its hold on the West Coast. Still, my attention wasn't on the temperature or the road conditions as my dad drove to the airport. Instead, I was preoccupied with replaying the visit and panning it for memories. I searched for something that was worth telling my mom, but came up empty. I wanted more time. I wasn't ready to go home yet. I needed one real moment with my dad first.

I got my wish. In a really sick, twisted way I received exactly what I wanted. As a result, we had a moment that changed our relationship forever. There are thousands of clichés (at least) about how things change so quickly . . . *in a snap, on a dime, in an instant.* Well, sometimes that's how things work. In flashes. They seem like they should be small, insignificant little things, but they're not. Or at least they aren't to me. Whether I made too much out of it, I'll let you decide. Regardless, my life was never the same again.

We arrived at the airport and discovered my flight was delayed and I couldn't leave until the next morning. Suddenly, time wasn't an issue anymore. I turned to my dad with a goofy grin on my face. I was ecstatic . . . for all of three seconds. Then I saw his expression. He looked like he'd been told he had a cavity or a button had popped off his favorite suit jacket. Mild annoyance set in to his weak jaw and disappointment settled in his eyes. There was no wild hug, no profession of happiness at this unexpected bounty. Was I hoping for too much? I don't think so. A little enthusiasm was more than in order, right?

In that moment, that instant, all his former declarations of love felt hollow and empty. The car ride back to his place passed in silence. There was only one question on my mind: *had he* ever *loved me?* I was too afraid of the answer to ask. When my dad finally spoke, it was only to say we needed to return to the airport the next morning early enough to buy breakfast with my vouchers. Upon arriving at his apartment, he turned the couch into a makeshift bed, gave me a hug goodnight, and disappeared into his room.

I didn't sleep that night. Every time I closed my eyes, I saw my dad's face as he realized my flight was delayed, so I burrowed deeper into the blankets and read. Books had always helped me escape before, and I hoped they wouldn't fail me now. I underestimated the power my dad had over me. As the hours marched on, my eyes began drifting from the pages, and his expression came crashing back in flashes. It was like a twisted version of Morse code that brought nothing but pain. Disappointment. *Keep looking at the words.* Never loved me. *Turn the page, Marni. Just flip it over.* What did I do wrong? *Don't think, Marni. Just read.* How can I make it better? *Read!* When had it changed? *READ, MARNI! JUST READ!*

Shadows fell in the room by the light of a single lamp. Everything felt gloomy and dark. I had always loved the rain and considered it the coziest form of weather imaginable, but alone in my dad's living room that night, it just made me feel insignificant. I started having strange, uneven thoughts. Death was on my mind, hazy and nebulous. Always the flashing continued. I began to cry, quiet tears at first that I hiccupped into the scratchy blankets while I hugged my books tighter. The flashes were undeniable, and the disappointment irreconcilable. My crying grew louder. Hesitantly, I called out for my dad. I wanted him to do everything he hadn't before—to place his arms around me and never let me go. Tears streamed down my face as I called "Dad?" plaintively into the silence. I was afraid to move from the couch. The shadows were too ominous for me to risk it. So I continued calling into the darkness for him.

I don't know how many hours I spent that way, terrified of the dark, and the truth, and the shadows, calling for my father. When he did come at last, I was exhausted. What he said, what I said, I can't recall. I know I didn't ask him if he loved me. The dream was better than nothing at all.

My dad's actions had troubled me for years but had been a jumbled puzzle before that night. I knew I had the pieces, but I hadn't been able to see the big picture. His disappointed look made everything click into place. I didn't like what lay before me, but at least I could recognize what I was up against. I waved good-bye to him as I boarded the plane, unaware of just how differently I would think of him the next time we saw each other.

The flight back home was a disaster. The plane sat on the runway for hours, waiting for the fog to lift. I munched on pretzels and tried to stop the flashing. It was only when I was well into the flight that I finally found relief through sleep. When I woke up, my personal issues were eclipsed by confusion and disorientation. The fog that had kept me in Los Angeles was still thwarting my journey home.

"So, the weather condition on the ground is preventing us from landing in Medford," the pilot announced calmly over the speakers. "We are circling above the airport right now so we can land if the fog clears. If it doesn't, we will have to land in Eugene. We apologize for this inconvenience and hope that the rest of the flight will be as pleasant as possible."

I felt nauseous. The pretzels I had consumed earlier were not agreeing with me. The plane continued circling while I kept flashing. I wanted to be home with an intensity I had rarely felt before. I needed my mom. I needed her to tell me everything would be okay. And she was just out of reach.

The fog didn't lift. By the time we landed at the Eugene airport, I was feeling more than a little loopy. The flight, the salt, the fear . . . it had all left me befuddled. Fortunately, I had the airport staff to take me under their wing and propel me behind closed doors. I was frog-marched to a small waiting area where I sat while my travel arrangements were made.

It wasn't a pretty room. The fluorescent lighting was obnoxious and made everything look unhealthily pale. I remember fake potted plants that I tried to avoid throwing up on. The room did have one considerable distraction:

Snickers. There were shelves full of them, box upon box of the delicious substance. I considered crossing the room and popping the treat into my mouth. *They wouldn't miss just one,* I rationalized, but I couldn't bring myself to do it. Instead, I kept hoping they would offer. In my head, it played out like this:

ME: Thank you so much for all your help.

AIRPORT PERSON: No problem. Is there anything we can do for you? Would you like a Snickers bar? They're really tasty.

ME: Are you sure you wouldn't mind?

AIRPORT PERSON: Absolutely.

[Camera zooms in to a close-up of the candy bar being unwrapped before focusing on my expression as I take a bite. My entire face relaxes as I enjoy the chocolaty goodness. Eyes roll back in appreciation.]

That didn't happen. Instead, I was hustled away from the room and loaded onto a bus with the other people from my flight. My queasiness refused to ease up, and it was only when a nice man noting my tense shoulders and worried face gave me half a croissant that things began to get better. I spent the rest of the bus ride peacefully watching the animated *George of the Jungle*. The movie did what the books had not: paused the flashes.

Three-and-a-half hours later, I was in Medford, where my mom scooped me into her arms and hugged me every bit as fiercely as I hugged her. In that moment, I knew everything would be okay. It didn't matter that my dad didn't really love me, that he didn't really want to get to know me, or that Richard was in the house. I had my mom and, as far as I was concerned, that was pretty damn good.

Chapter 6

MIDDLE SCHOOL IS HELL. Actually, that's a lie. It isn't hell. It's far worse. After all, no religion sentences people to a sinkhole where *hormones* run rampant. I'm not the only one who feels this way, either. It's one of those universally acknowledged truths. In middle school, the popular kids seem to float effortlessly while the dweebs (aka me) just struggle to keep their heads above water. I hated everything about the place, from my locker, which had been cleverly designed to never open for me, to my teacher, who had no sympathy for those of us who happened to be mathematically challenged. Everything felt painfully mediocre. My brown hair felt browner, my stomach rounder, and my sweatshirts uglier. It just sort of happened.

The only thing worse than my first day of sixth grade was the second day, which confirmed my suspicion that it wasn't going to get any better. My teacher, Mrs. P., was insane. Not "ha-ha, you're so eccentric/unique/charming" insane, either. Nope. She was a staunch believer in "tough love" who had declared war on all forms of "coddling." In actuality, she was annihilating all displays of understanding and empathy. To that effect, she devised a system. Whenever someone needed help, she would listen without eye contact before she produced one loud, crisp, humiliating, mortifying word: *bummer*. That single word took up the space of thousands and gained extra syllables as it reverberated around the room. Somehow, it became *BUM-MMM-ER!* One woman alone could never create the necessary force for this to happen, which is why the whole class joined in. Humiliation really isn't complete unless everyone is actively involved.

Middle school did help me develop one magical skill. That was the power of invisibility. Considering I practiced disappearing every school day, five days a week, my success isn't all that remarkable. Once I mastered the technique, it wasn't as difficult as I had anticipated. I just kept my head down, avoided the girls' locker room, had minimal social interaction, and hid in the library. This kept me shielded from Mrs. P., but didn't exactly make me popular. In fact, I became "that girl." You know, the one who eats lunch in the library every day in her bulky sweatshirts. The one who only expresses herself in stilted sentences. Yeah. That was me.

I didn't even have Gwyn to lean on anymore. The two of us had a falling out right before we entered middle school and weren't on speaking terms. Actually, that isn't exactly right. I wasn't speaking to her. Not because I didn't miss her or still like her. I just felt like with all her popularity, she didn't care about me. I didn't want to be clinging to someone who didn't value me. That isn't all that happened between the two of us to end the friendship. I had a flash with Gwyn too. I was on the ground, having just managed to fall off a low tree branch, and Gwyn looked at me with complete unconcern. Instead of thinking her reaction was because I wasn't hurt, I took it as a sign that she didn't care about what happened to me. That's the problem with flashes. When they are right, they are convenient, but when they are wrong, they bring about horrible misunderstandings. Luckily, I was able to figure out this particular error of mine before it was too late. Unluckily, I was out of middle school by the time I did.

Without Gwyn, my life was seriously lonely. She had been my best friend for as long as I could remember, and I felt lost without her by my side. Trying to make sense of a Gwyn-free world that included Mrs. P., the middle-school social scene, my inability to understand math, and my family problems, I ended up in therapy. In hindsight, I am only surprised it didn't happen sooner.

Deep down, I think I always knew the decision to seek professional help was the right one. It took me awhile to work up the nerve to explain it to my mom. I didn't come right out and say, "Hey, Mom, guess what? My life sucks, and I need professional help so I can stop living like a social pariah. Oh, and so I can figure out how to deal with Dad. How was your day?" So instead, I just told her the truth about how I was feeling. I explained that I went around empty inside, like somewhere along the line the ability to love had been sucked out of me by an enormous vacuum. Coming from the mouth of a sixth-grader, my mom found it disturbing enough to take action, which is how I landed Carrie the Therapist.

I'm not ashamed of my time in therapy anymore, although when I first started going, I was embarrassed about it. I thought it was humiliating to be just starting middle school and already have a shrink. That's how I saw it, anyway. *I'm hardly here a week, and already I need a professional to fix me.* I couldn't bring myself to tell anyone but my mom about my sessions. The whole family knew I was going, but I still wanted to keep it quiet. If anyone asked about my plans during a therapy session time, I casually said I had "an appointment," before scurrying away. Despite the fact that I thought therapy consigned me to a lifetime of loserdom, I kept going regularly because I knew it was good for me. I *had* to talk things out. My only regret is that my therapist was Carrie.

Carrie was nothing if not consistent. She always brought her clients into a small, windowless room with two chairs and a sandbox. She settled down in the one chair that was remotely comfortable before telling me to "express myself" with the sandbox, which is far more difficult than one might expect. I was instructed to "transfer my emotions" onto fig-urine animals that I then placed deliberately in the sand. Carrie watched all this and nodded her head expertly from time to time. Right before my mom was scheduled to pick me up, she examined the scene to interpret my inner angst.

"Are you the bird?" she asked me. "Does the fox represent your father?"

I replied that it did.

"See how the fox is creeping up on the bird? I think you're worried your dad is going to hurt you out of the blue."

I was amazed because she was right. I *did* worry that my dad would crush my heart. I already felt so empty. I was afraid that if I suffered any more pain, I'd be impossible to put back together again. So I nodded and stewed over my relationship with my dad until our next session. In hindsight, I can recognize that Carrie was not a good therapist. I never felt like she actually cared about me. I was sure if she did, she would have occasionally let me sit in the one non-lousy chair. I sort of resented that.

I don't think Carrie deserves credit for my growth—I never would have improved if it hadn't been for my mom. The best part of my therapy sessions, the only part I looked forward to, was the drive to Carrie's office. It took well over a half an hour, and my mom and I were the only people in the car. I never went through a "rebellious teenager" phase that made me shun my mother. In fact, middle school just made me want to open up to her more than ever before. The best part of my day was always retelling it once I returned home. We discussed everything, from the boys I was crushing on to my inability to comprehend basic mathematics. How I hated Dad. How I missed him anyway.

My mom didn't try to be my therapist. Maybe that's why she was so helpful. She didn't need to look into a sandbox to understand what was going on. Instead, she listened, laughed, commiserated, and gave me advice. Talking to her gave me more peace of mind than any session with Carrie. When it was just the two of us, we were free. I didn't have to try to make a good impression or disappear. She didn't have to worry about Richard and keeping everyone happy. It was a chance to let go of worldly pressures.

Our home certainly wasn't a refuge from trouble and stress. Especially not with Richard trying to be a combination of therapist/friend/father/role model. He saw me as a challenging puzzle that he wanted credit for putting back together. Richard decided the fastest way for me to become self-actualized was to concentrate on my relationship with my dad. He prodded me until I cried. Richard believed tears were the only reliable sign that therapy was working. Obligingly, I wailed and moaned and felt like a complete and total fake, which only made me feel emptier in the end.

Not that I didn't have plenty of provocation to cry over my dad. Our relationship had disintegrated to the point of nonexistence. I wasn't cute anymore, which meant I could no longer squeeze into little velvet dresses and go to bar or bat mitzvah parties. My inability to turn down chocolate chip cookies meant that he no longer wanted to parade me in front of strangers, which was fine by me since I'd always hated the social awkwardness and pageantry. The awful part was that he just sort of . . . left. We never spoke on the phone and we never e-mailed. He wasn't necessarily trying to cut me out, but he didn't care enough to keep me.

I tried to stay connected with him and overlook the truth. I remember receiving a letter from him on my birthday. I was bursting with excitement because I hadn't heard from him in ages. Smiling broadly, I tore open the letter expecting to see well wishes and proclamations of love. Even if I knew they weren't real, I could have pretended he still loved me. What I found inside was a magazine clipping about inventions made by kids with a hastily scribbled postscript that just said "Happy Birthday." There wasn't even a card inside. He called that night and asked if I had gotten his letter. For a second, I hoped he was going to tell me he had sent two letters and the other one had a card with a bear holding a birthday balloon. He didn't. Instead, he chatted about the stupid inventions before hanging up. I remember turning to my mom and bursting into tears. There was no real card, no real call, and no real present from Dad that year. That became the birthday trend.

Still, I did everything I could to preserve what little we had. After discussing it with Carrie, I called up my dad and let him have it. I told him how hurt I was and how much I wanted him to be in my life. I pleaded that he do the flying for a change and come see me. I flat-out begged. He turned me down. He said he couldn't come back to Ashland because of "all the memories it brought up." I pointed out that since

I was there we could create new, happy memories. He still refused. I gave him an ultimatum: either he hop on a flight within the next four months or I wouldn't speak to him. I thought for sure that would propel him into action. Once again, I was wrong. The months passed with no sign of him. I was rejected by my own father. It wasn't to be the last time he broke me.

Chapter 7

THE BEST THING ABOUT Richard was that suddenly I had a male figure in my life. I had someone to take me fishing. I didn't even like fishing, but that didn't matter. I had a fishing buddy who wanted me to be out on the lake with him. Someone besides my mom was telling me that I was a great girl. I couldn't really believe it, but I never minded hearing him say it.

History does repeat itself. Or at the very least, it echoes a lot. Once again, I was the favorite. Like my dad, Richard preferred me to my siblings, and he wreaked havoc with the house. This time, Jordan got the brunt of it. The two of them jockeyed for alpha male position until Jordan up and left. I understand why he moved out. In his position, I would have done the same. Jonathan, Shayna, and I could cope with

Richard by staying away from him when he was feeling moody. We didn't need Jordan to protect us. I'm not so sure Jordan realized that—I suspect he felt like he was abandoning us. I could be very wrong, but I do know that ever since then, Jordan has tried to act like a father to me. He counsels and advises until I want to smack him and demand he be my brother for a change.

None of that mattered at the time, though. Jordan was gone, and Richard ruled the house. The other problem was that my mom wasn't happy. Richard kept her emotionally stifled and artistically repressed by critiquing everything she did, searching for flaws. He pretended this was to "help her grow." I suspect he was afraid of what would happen if my mom reached her full potential, that she would realize she didn't need their relationship and leave him.

Even if Richard hadn't been there to put a damper on my home life, I probably still would have been depressed. Therapy can't fix everything, and my loneliness persisted. My school life was miserable, my social life nonexistent, and my family falling apart at the seams. I hadn't been able to make things better with Shayna—she still hated my guts. The rift between us was too deep and old to be overcome. It didn't matter that I understood Dad now too. Nothing changed between Shayna and me, even when I officially severed all contact with Dad. The two of us had been raised as rivals, and the presence or absence of Dad couldn't change that.

I didn't know who I was. My mom pointed out that she was in her forties and was still puzzling it out. This fact didn't strike me as comforting. Middle school was supposed to be a magical time when your true identity could be uncovered. That isn't how it actually worked. The only thing I knew was that I repulsed myself. I hated everything: my antisocial ways, my body, even my hate. I walked around the halls of Ashland Middle School with a pool of venom inside. I didn't know where I belonged, so I holed up in the school library and focused on reading books. It seemed like the safest thing to do.

I don't think I was ever truly suicidal, although there were times when I thought death might be preferable to the emptiness of my life. At those times, I'd walk into the kitchen to look at our knives. There was something coldly appealing about the shiny, black handles that jutted out of the rack. The knowledge that I could end it, make all of it disappear, sank in as I stared, transfixed by the possibility in the flashing metal.

I only came close to taking action once.

I've never been much of an artist. Not in any one field, anyway. I sort of dabbled in one thing before I checked out something else. Consequently, there are only a handful of art projects I've ever made that are anything special. In fifth grade, I created something spectacular. It came out of nowhere. One second I was making a pastel drawing of a toucan, and the next, a bird was knowingly looking back at me. He (the bird was very clear on the matter of his gender) was an unexpected present. He was also one of the few things that Shayna complimented, which in my eyes instantly propelled him to Mona Lisa status. I lovingly posted him to my door so we could look at each other every day. My toucan became a daily reminder that I hadn't always been in middle school. He pointed out that I had actually enjoyed school once before and could do it again. He was far more to me than paper and pastel—he was a friend. One of my only friends. It was the attack of the toucan that almost drove me to kill myself.

Shayna was mad at me for some reason, which was nothing new. I was always doing something to set her off. Just breathing appeared to be enough to send her into a rage. This made it hard to know if I had screwed up or if Shayna just felt like yelling at me. Shayna and I also had very different perspectives on right and wrong. Leaving a bowl to soak in the sink a little too long wasn't a big deal in my opinion. For her, it was a hanging offense. Anyhow, she confronted me late one night about my most recent transgression. She was ranting about something I had failed to do while I tried to tune her out. I remember thinking it was one of those times where she just felt like screaming. I knew it'd be best to nod and wait it out, but for some reason, I couldn't. It was late, the house was silent (with the exception of her ranting), and I just wanted to go to sleep. I flat-out didn't have the energy for an emotional roller coaster. So, after she had gotten most of the rant out of her system, I asked her to leave.

What happened next, I'd like to forget. Shayna became livid and continued yelling until she stalked over to my door. Whipping it open, she clenched her hand into a fist and proceeded to mutilate my toucan. She beat upon the door, smudging the bird with the single mechanical purpose of a semi-automatic: to destroy. For me, it was the shot heard round the world. It brought me to a level of hysteria.

I scrambled to rescue my toucan. Pastels are designed to smudge and create a blending effect. While his eyes didn't stare at me as brightly, he wasn't completely ruined. His long shapely beak, brightly-colored plumage, and sturdy torso all remained perfectly preserved. None of that struck me as important, as it was a mere technicality. I was staring at a bird of a different feather. My toucan had never known hate or anger. He had been raised in a happy bubble world just like me. Shayna's fist had destroyed that, and there was no going back. My toucan was gone forever.

Shayna's icy gaze never left my face. I remember wondering vaguely how eyes could turn so flat and cold without creating frostbite. Maybe she was protected from the chill by the seething hate that burned in her throat.

"When you die, Marni," she said deliberately, "no one will come to your funeral."

She left after that. I don't think she could have invented a harsher parting shot. At first, all I could do was stare at the toucan and apologize to it. I told him that I had wanted to keep him safe. I never meant to put him in harm's way. That wasn't enough to distract me from Shayna's final words. In fact, the toucan only seemed to confirm that I wouldn't be missed. I let everyone down. I couldn't even be trusted to keep an inanimate object as a friend. I wracked my brain for names, for faces, for anyone who would care if I were to disappear. The list I produced was pathetically small (with no birds). It didn't even include my dad. I figured he couldn't miss something that wasn't in his life. He'd be able to move on without too much trouble. My mom would have a harder time dealing with the loss. "But what would she lose?" I wondered aloud. "What on earth would she miss? Shayna is smart. Jordan is charming. Jonathan is athletic. What do I bring to the table?

Nothing." I spiraled downward, lost in self-loathing and pity.

I started talking to God that night. Don't worry, he didn't answer. I didn't find religion in my moment of crisis. That only happens in movies. I don't even know if what I was doing could be considered talking. I was muttering accusations and demanding answers. I threw out all my questions to the silence. I asked whether it was better to be entirely dead than to keep living with death inside, whether an empty heart trumped a broken one.

I went to the kitchen and forced my shaking hands to pull out a knife. Spoiler alert: I didn't do it. I guess that doesn't come as much of a surprise. Instead, I had a miniature epiphany. Not a godly or a magical one. There were no celestial choirs instructing me. It was a very down-to-earth, well-isn't-that-obvious moment of enlightenment. As I held the glittering knife, I suddenly realized the magnitude of the act . . . there were no do-overs. I couldn't die, realize my mistake, and rejoin the land of the living. Once I used the knife, it was game over. I would have my funeral and probably prove Shayna right. That's what made me stop. I needed to make sure her prophecy never came true. I needed to find people to attend my funeral.

If this seems petty and small, all I have to say in my defense is that sometimes that's how life-altering epiphanies work. That night, I resolved to change other people's lives. I wanted to be on the dedication page of someone else's book. I wanted to be the I-couldn't-have-done-it-without-you person. The one who made all the difference. If that could be me, I decided, they'd have to buy Kleenex in bulk and airlift it in for my funeral.

I never really considered suicide again. Not just because of my determination to fill my funeral with mourners, but because I realized that I'm worth saving too. Sure, I make a lot of mistakes (and have a tendency to humiliate myself), but that's part of my charm. That's what makes me Marni. That's one thing I should never change. Life is just more interesting with me in it—especially when I've got no idea what I am doing.

Chapter 8

I LOVE MY SISTER. I know it sounds like I don't (or perhaps that I shouldn't), but I love my sister. I always will. This doesn't mean I don't realize we have a twisted relationship. It'd be great if we could see each other without descending to snarky comments and backhanded insults. Somehow, I doubt it's going to change anytime soon. The crazy thing is, despite our inability to express our love, it's still there. Under all the anger and frustration is a whole lot of love. I had a hard time believing that as a kid. I understood the concept of a loving relationship and a hate-filled one. I just didn't get that something could really be both. I never realized that when Shayna yelled at me for talking to strangers it was because she was horribly afraid someone would take advantage of me. It wasn't until years later that Shayna confided her biggest fear was that I would be raped. *That* is caring. That is part of the reason I will love her no matter what she says or does (although I might not like her a lot sometimes). It was fortunate for me that situations arose that revealed true affection. Our trip to Costa Rica was one such occasion.

Grandma Joyce invited all of us on a trip to celebrate her birthday. I wasn't sure I wanted to go. I didn't know if I was ready to deal with my dad. I'd come to the conclusion that he was a lousy human being, and I didn't want that confirmed again on the trip. The idea of going back to Costa Rica was very enticing, however. I thought that maybe if I went with all my siblings, it would work out all right. I figured it would be a lot harder for my dad to mess with my head with Jordan, Jonathan, and Shayna present to set the record straight. Part of me was also hoping that with my therapy, I was mature enough to form a connection with my dad. I wanted to be able to deal with him like my brothers did—in a sort of cool, professional manner. A relationship based on an impersonal exchange of niceties sounded like a great solution to me. Maybe it would have been, if I hadn't hoped for more. As it was, I overestimated my ability to remain detached.

The first bad omen was the rental car. Technically, there was nothing wrong with it. It started, stopped, and turned.

It behaved like a perfectly normal, nonpossessed car. The problem lay in its size, which, for the record, matters. It might have been perfect for an intimate honeymoon trip, but for a large family vacation it was a nightmare. My dad tried to argue his way into a bigger one, arms flapping and head bobbing in his best chicken impersonation, but failed.

There was really nothing for me to do but sit in the sweltering heat. I had nothing to distract me from the sensation that the plastic seat was melting into me. My mom thought it would be best if I didn't lug my CD player to Costa Rica. Meanwhile, Jonathan and Shayna had their headphones on while Jordan tried to sort out the problem. Not that Jordan had any luck, since my dad refused to listen to him. Everything (even the arrangement of the suitcases) had to be done my dad's way. So, there we were: squeezed and squashed within an inch of our lives in the rental. The heat made everyone surly and smelly as we bumped along the road to our hotel.

This is a good time to point out that many roads in Costa Rica aren't so great. They come with potholes. Lots and lots of potholes. Our suitcases served as seatbelts, but made me feel like an arcade game pinball being buffeted from all sides. Even so, driving in Costa Rica would have been bearable if it hadn't been for the orange juice.

We were a day into our trip when the OJ came up in conversation. Grandma Joyce wanted to know if we wanted anything from the all-purpose convenience store. Her timing couldn't have been worse, since we were in the middle of a particularly uncomfortable meal. My dad was sulking about something—possibly his inability to get a bigger car—and was in no mood to be pleasant. He was glowering at the table when Grandma Joyce broke the silence.

"So, does anyone want anything special for the morning?" she asked.

My siblings and I traded looks. All we wanted was to go home. Or keep traveling without the two of them.

"I think we're fine," said Jordan, taking on the role of spokesman.

"Are you sure?" she pressed. Grandma Joyce, like her son, was primarily led by what was in her best interests. In this case, she wanted to buy juice but make it look like she was doing us a favor.

"We're sure," Jordan assured her.

"What about orange juice?"

None of us really liked orange juice. We never drank it at home. We had some in the refrigerator, but it was used primarily for my mom's sludge-like concoction of orange juice, ice, and Diet Coke.

"We don't want orange juice," Jordan replied politely.

"You say that now," she wheedled, "but tomorrow you'll be saying you want it and complaining that we don't have any." She said the last bit like she understood fickle teenagers better than we did. But she didn't know us. She didn't have a clue as to what we were really like. If she had, she wouldn't have asked us about orange juice in the first place. It was therefore up to Jordan to try to educate her.

"We don't want orange juice," Jordan repeated. There was no way to make our position clearer. We were anti-orange juice.

"But . . ." was as far as she got. My dad, who had been growing increasingly angry as the conversation progressed, had reached his limit.

"They said they don't want orange juice!" he barked.

Silence descended.

Grandma Joyce muttered a few choice words about kids' inability to make up their minds. She mumbled that soon, very soon, we would have a change of heart. The meal ended with the tension more palpable than the food.

The orange juice incident would have ended there had she not bought a whole carton. As expected, she was the only one who wanted to drink any of it, which only led to more juice-related conflict the next morning. She tried to convince everyone that we were secretly craving orange juice. If drug dealers guilt-tripped and pressured people the way my Grandma Joyce did, the streets would be a lot more dangerous.

We declined the orange juice. It felt like a matter of principle. She thought she knew us better than we did, and the only way to prove her wrong was not to drink it. All of us ignored the orange juice. This left her with an almost-full carton to transport via pathetically small rental car to our next hotel in Costa Rica, which is where the real trouble began.

I didn't actually hear the conversation between Grandma Joyce and my dad. I'm guessing she told him to be careful of potholes so as not to spill the juice. That's mere conjecture though. It was hot in the car—a steamy, sweaty hot that left me feeling languid and tired. I rested my head against the window and wished myself somewhere else.

WHAM!

My dad slammed on the breaks, and we were thrown forward onto suitcases. The jolt was followed by cursing and sharp intakes of breath. I gasped and rubbed my stomach where the corner of something had jabbed me. Jordan, Jonathan, and Shayna repositioned themselves beneath their loads, muttering darkly.

I stared in disbelief at the back of my dad's head. He hadn't stopped because there was some rare lizard crossing the road or anything. He had done it because of the orange juice. More specifically, because he was mad at Grandma Joyce for mentioning it.

He yelled something and started the car again before any of us had even caught our breaths. The car had just started moving steadily when Grandma Joyce opened her mouth. She just couldn't resist.

WHAM!

The second lurch sent Jordan into action. He shoved the boxes off him, wrenched open the door, climbed out, and marched over to my dad in the driver's seat. Leaning past him, Jordan snatched up the orange juice, opened the carton and deliberately poured every last drop onto the nearest plant.

I think everyone has moments in life when they get to show what they're really made of, and that was one of Jordan's. He refused to be tossed around in the car over orange juice, so he ended it. As I watched him dump out the juice, I saw an act of rebellion every bit as big as the Boston Tea Party. It was comforting watching Jordan take care of everything, especially since I couldn't count on my dad to do the right thing.

Believe it or not, the orange juice helped me bond with my siblings. Adversity either brings people together or wrenches them apart. Stuck in a foreign country with

Grandma Joyce and my dad made Shayna and me closer. It created a truce between us while we focused on making it out of there with our sanity intact. Presenting a united front was the only way to survive. It also proved once and for all that we loved each other.

I remember one night in particular when the love wasn't hidden between us. It started with my dad giving Shayna an extra hard time. We finished eating, and Shayna was ready to return to the hotel. Dad refused to give her the room key, saying she wasn't mature enough to handle the responsibility. This was ridiculous. Walking a few blocks to a hotel doesn't require much maturity. What it does need is a level head and a sense of direction. Shayna had those qualities, as well as his required maturity, in spades. Everyone tried to explain the idiocy behind this position, but he remained firm. It was only when Jonathan announced his intention to join us that he budged. He handed the key to Jonathan, and the three of us marched out of the restaurant.

It was dark and quiet as we walked along the street. It felt good to move and hear the sound of my footsteps reverberating with theirs. We felt so close, so united, that nothing could tear us apart. Jonathan took out the room key and awkwardly offered it to Shayna. Jonathan was interesting like that—he could be a major pain, but when someone was hurt, he'd always try to fix it. He wanted to show Shayna that he trusted her with the key—that *he* knew my dad was wrong. Shayna didn't take the key. I think it was sort of her toucan. If my dad had just handed it to her, that would have meant something. Now, it was just a reminder that she was still untrusted and unloved. This time she wasn't alone in her anger at Dad. Jonathan and I were just as sick of his self-centered ways and commiserated as we walked shoulder-to-shoulder. That's when I began swearing.

I started with the classics. I used every word I'd heard in the middle-school hallways that I'd decided never to repeat. I loved it and felt a surge of power as the words rolled off my tongue and filled the chilly night air with nothing but the dulcet sound of my profanity.

Shayna and Jonathan were shocked. They'd never really heard me swear before. In fact, I'm not sure I ever had. My mom had kept me sheltered as a kid, and that had lasted longer than she probably expected. Growing up on happy-go-lucky musicals like *Singin' in the Rain* had made me a stranger to the world of profanity. The words felt strange on my tongue, and I was caught by surprise at the hatred that spilled out. That night, my dad became an infection and swearing the only possible antidote. There was a sort of poetry to it too. It wasn't elegant or profound, but it was beautiful.

The walk back to the hotel that night was one of the best strolls of my life. Sure, it felt like the world was in cahoots with my dad, but I had my siblings on my side. I wouldn't have traded teams if he offered me the world. I sensed Jonathan's concern for me. As a little kid, Jonathan used to be my protector. I was too young to remember, but apparently he guarded me from the others and watched over me diligently. I wish I could recall those times. Even though he had moved on to spending all his time either closed up in his room or on the tennis court with his friends, I guess some things don't change. Not that he would want to own up to his softer side. He was always secretly sweet and guarded his kindness fiercely, as if afraid someone would catch him in the act and tease him about it. At the end of the day though, I knew we still had a connection. I could hear it in his voice when he called me a "dorkus maximus."

Alongside Jonathan's concern was something akin to appreciation coming from Shayna. In that split second, it was as if our history didn't matter, as if I was forgiven for being his former favorite. We were no longer rivals but allies. It was partly born out of necessity, since we had both agreed to spend a few extra days in Los Angeles with him after Costa Rica. I think there was more to it than a survival instinct, though. We had a moment, and that was what mattered to me. My favorite memory from the trip wasn't swimming with dolphins, or river rafting, or any of the things that fill up travel brochures. It was the memory of an empty orange juice container and a night of swearing with my siblings at my side. They weren't traditional Kodak moments, but for me, they were better. So I sort of have my dad to thank for that . . . and nothing else.

Chapter 9

COSTA RICA WAS GORGEOUS, and even the presence of my dad and Grandma Joyce couldn't diminish it. Everything was lush and green and overflowing with life. Ironically, it sort of reminded me of Ashland. Or maybe I just thought that because I was homesick. I missed my mom, and after the heat, the insects, the crabs running under my bed, I felt like I'd had my share of the exotic. I was ready to return. Unbeknownst to me, we were going to be taking a lot of Costa Rica with us.

My dad decided to bring coffee back to the states for his clients, which sounded reasonable to me. The last time we had gone to Costa Rica, my dad had been excited about bringing home coffee. He had dragged me to a place where they roasted it right in front of the customers. The smell of coffee was so strong it stung my eyes, and I had to wait outside to catch my breath. So, I didn't think it was unusual in any way that he wanted to get some coffee this time too. Frankly, I wouldn't have cared, had he been able to restrain himself. He purchased 100 pounds of it.

There is really nothing you can say when someone does something like that. One second, we were all waiting in the rental car for him and the next he approached with a stranger wheeling 100 pounds of Vanilla Blend, a big, foolish grin plastered all over his smarmy face.

Our first question, quite naturally, was *What was he thinking?* There wasn't enough room in the rental car without the coffee—the last thing we needed was more cargo. When we pointed that out, he just shrugged his shoulders (still grinning) and said, "You'll have to make more room." Gee, thanks.

By the time we reached the airport, none of us ever wanted to see our father again. We were at the point of mutiny when we boarded the flight. The boys were lucky enough to be going straight home, which left Shayna and me wishing we'd never agreed to stay a few extra days in California. For once, Shayna wasn't my biggest problem. Until we were out of enemy territory, the truce had to remain intact.

This might not be fair, but I would like to blame *The Far Side, Calvin and Hobbes,* and Richard for the next disaster. I'm sure this has a fancy clinical name like blame transference, and that a therapist would point out it is not a particularly productive way of dealing with things. Still, it would be nice to have someone other than my dad to hold responsible.

Dad took Shayna and me to a used bookstore under the pretext of "bonding." He wasn't fooling anyone. Once inside, he went straight to the geology section and never left it. Shayna checked out their selection of romance novels, and I decided to examine the comic books. Richard loved comics, so I thought buying him a few might make a nice present. Of course, this unselfish little act helped me out quite a bit too. When Richard was happy, he didn't sulk around the house like a peevish ghost. So, I approached my dad a few hours later with several books tucked under one arm. He was carrying a stack that was as enormous as it was impractical. He had geology books written in French, a language he couldn't speak or read. Yet, for some strange reason, he felt compelled to own these books. I decided not to comment on it and instead added my comic books to the pile.

My dad could never pass up a deal, and apparently the bookstore had a promotion—an extra discount for purchasing 100 dollars worth of books. In order to reach the magic number, he harassed me into grabbing a few more comic books. He kept telling me what a good deal it was, which would have been nice if he were footing the bill. He wasn't. He fully expected me to pay him back for every penny. Back at his house, we realized that was a problem because I didn't have the cash. Jonathan had offered to transport most of my money back to Ashland for safekeeping. So, even after I'd checked every pocket in every article of clothing I owned, I still had a five-dollar deficit.

Five measly bucks. Less than a tall Mocha Frappuccino and a pumpkin loaf from Starbucks, and my dad wouldn't let it go. Instead, he demanded I mail it to him from Ashland. *Seriously*. When I told him that wasn't going to happen, he took to bugging Shayna. Why didn't she loan me the money? She was my sister after all, it was only right that she look after my debts. He even started making bargains in my name, offering to exchange cash if I did her chores for a week or more.

Shayna refused, while I watched him in disbelief.

"Dad," I pointed out reasonably. "You haven't sent me a birthday present, a Hanukkah present . . . *anything*, for years. I haven't even gotten a *card* from you! Why don't you put the five dollars towards that?"

He rounded on me.

"I take you to Costa Rica, and the first thing you do is hit me up for money! I'm not made out of it, you know!"

This coming from a man who bought 100 pounds of coffee and dozens of geology books written in French.

"Grandma Joyce paid for the trip," I countered. "And we're talking about five dollars here. I haven't seen you in well over a year. This shouldn't be a problem!"

But for my dad, any money not in his bank account was a problem.

"I paid for half of that trip, and I am not giving you the money," he insisted.

We parted ways with a lackluster goodbye, and I took the comic books and the five-dollar debt home with me. Leaving was a relief, and the only sad part was the way my solidarity with Shayna crumbled the second we landed in Medford. I was back to being the little sister she wanted to avoid. Still, at least I had my mom. Much to my surprise, I also had Richard suggesting a way to exact payback.

He got the whole thing set up for me. It didn't require much equipment: wood boards, strong glue, sandpaper, and 500 pennies. The rest was up to me. Painstakingly, I sandpapered one side of each penny and neatly glued them in sets of 100 to slabs of wood. It was supposed to be the ultimate slap in the face. I owed him five dollars, and this way he would get every single penny of it back. The only catch was that it, rather like him, would be absolutely worthless. The whole act was rich in symbolic meaning, and I knew I could never have thought up such an intricate way to say "screw you" on my own.

I would love to think of my pennies as a huge success. In a movie, I think it would have played out really well and been very dramatic. I would've waited to deliver the pennies in person. Around midnight, I would've walked the handful of blocks that separated my grandparents' house from his and leaned on the doorbell until he showed up. Then I would've shoved the boards into his face and told him what I really thought—that he was a lousy father who had put his children through hell. That I wouldn't cry at his funeral.

In reality, my life wasn't quite that dramatic. Or maybe it was, and I was too much of a chicken to go through with it. I couldn't even bring myself to face him.

The next time I was in Los Angeles, I stayed in the safety of my grandparents' house and refused to see him. My brothers went instead and played basketball with him. That was the easiest way for them to spend time with my dad without becoming irritated by him. If they were concentrating on dribbling, guarding, and shooting, they didn't really have to talk. I chose not to talk at all and just enjoy spending time with grandma and grandpa. The pennies were burning a hole in my suitcase though, and I knew I had to send them to him. I didn't want to owe my father anything. I wanted to pay up, close shop, and walk away.

I considered dropping the pennies off at his house in the night and just leaving. In the end, I took the wimpy way out and asked Jordan to deliver them for me. He didn't really want to do it. He looked me squarely in the eyes and with brotherly concern asked if I knew what I was doing, if I understood the message I was sending. He was concerned I wasn't prepared to deal with the consequences of my first act of teenage rebellion. I replied confidently that I knew exactly what my pennies were saying. In hindsight, I think perhaps I was mistaken, not for sending the pennies, making the pennies, the sentiment behind the pennies, or my ability to deal with my dad's reaction, especially because he saw it as one big joke. No, I think it might have been a mistake because it wasn't about my father or me. It was all about Richard. He liked dramatic acts of vengeance, and I knew he would be proud of me if I did it. Once again I was pandering to the man in my life. My declaration of independence from my father didn't prove a thing. I still craved attention and love and was willing to sandpaper my hands to get it. I had a long way to go.

Chapter 10

I WISH I COULD SAY that middle school improved. However, in most respects, it didn't. I returned from Costa Rica to the same social problems I had left behind. I did, however, become craftier. I slowly figured out there are some areas only elite nerds (including myself) have access to that can be used to their advantage. Granted, this was behind the counter in the school library, but still, it came with perks. I could read all the newest books, check out tapes that weren't typically distributed, and turn in books late pretty much hassle-free. I saw this as a huge success. I was also invited to join the prestigious, if somewhat unknown, Ashland Middle School Book Club. I didn't care if this certified me as a dork. I was discussing intense novels like *Icy Sparks* (about one girl's battle with Tourette's syndrome) surrounded by other girls who liked to read. I was finally finding my niche.

The book club wasn't the only place I started fitting in. I soon joined the ranks of the "theater people." I worked my way up by starting at the very bottom in *Oliver!*, where I was cast as an orphan and had all of one line: "Stop him!" Backstage, I was part of a group that did tongue twisters and chanted "Whether the weather is cold, or whether the weather is hot, we'll be together whatever the weather, whether we like it or not." I always liked being with the group—especially when I met Natasha.

There are some people who can't help but change your life. Natasha was one of them for me. She was everything I wanted to be—thin, smart, pretty, talented, and even though she was homeschooled, universally adored. Much to my surprise, she was also my new best friend. We talked about everything: boys, music, and especially books. Our taste in young adult fiction was pretty much identical. We both loved Meg Cabot, Gordon Korman, and Tamora Pierce. We could (and did) discuss their various works for days. At long last, I had found someone I considered my intellectual equal, if not my superior. This isn't to say I thought the rest of the school was unintelligent or that I was above the other students. In most cases, I was the one who was negligently behind. My math skills were nonexistent and my social skills needed serious work. When it came to books though, I was pretty much in a league of my own. Until Natasha that is.

I did make it to seventh grade. I survived Mrs. P.'s *BUM-MMM-ER*s and a year's worth of indecision as to which boy I had the strongest crush on. Some days I told myself I wasn't interested in any of them. Usually, I imagined dating all of them. Somehow though, I made it past the "Marni likes Tyler" class camping trip (a truth I denied hotly . . . yeah, I was totally clueless) and onto the next level of middle school.

Seventh grade meant big changes. No longer would I be the recipient of the dreaded *BUM-MMM-ER* since I now had a different teacher for every subject. After holding my own as an orphan in *Oliver!* and as a singing tree in *Once on This Island,* I was given real roles in the school plays. Overall, these were major improvements, and I might have stayed in school if it hadn't been for my phys ed (P.E.) class and President John Adams.

P.E. was mandatory, and I had signed up for what I thought would be the least humiliating form of exercise—dance. I was horribly mistaken. Dance class didn't just embarrass me: it was an embarrassment to itself. The older, well-coordinated students took it upon themselves to teach the rest of us routines that were comprised of an "attitude" overdose and hip swishing, none of which I could do, not because I was humiliated (which I was), but because I had no coordination. I tripped my way through routines two-and-a-half beats behind everyone else. I decided the class couldn't get any more mortifying—which is when it did. We were ordered to create our own routine and perform it. In front of *everyone*.

I don't know anyone in their right mind who would look forward to something like that. Maybe if I looked more like Kirsten Dunst in *Bring It On* and less like Velma from *Scooby-Doo*, I wouldn't have dreaded it so much, though I sincerely doubt it. The very thought of doing a simple step ball change had my heart thudding and not in a happy adrenaline way, but in a *Jaws* something-very-bad-is-about-to-happen way. It wasn't just the dancing part that scared me—I had to pick the music as well. I knew that what I listened to wasn't cool. The best mainstream stuff I listened to was Chumbawamba (their song "Tubthumping" was the greatest thing ever). I quickly vetoed doing a number to that particular tune. I couldn't do hip-hop or rap without looking absolutely foolish. Primarily, I listened to pop music on *The Princess Diaries* soundtrack or oldies like Frank Sinatra. The idea of strutting around to "Supergirl" or "Ain't Nuthin' But a She Thing" sent me into a cold sweat.

But hip thrusts weren't enough to send me scurrying from

the middle school. Yes, they scared me into looking for alternatives, but I wouldn't actually have left if it hadn't been for John Adams. If you're wondering how a one-term president who died in the 1800s convinced me to become a dropout, you're not alone. I'm not entirely sure how he did it, either. Here's what I do know: I fell in love with John Adams.

Not romantically, of course. He's *dead,* and I am not the type to find that an attractive feature in a guy. I guess what I fell in love with was *learning* about John Adams. He was one seriously cool guy. Not only was he an unbelievably good lawyer (who represented the British after the Boston Massacre because, hey, everyone deserves good representation), he also convinced other countries to help bankroll the United States. Without him, the United States would have remained a backwater British colony. On top of all that, he committed political suicide by keeping the country out of war during his presidency. I guess you could say I became a fan. Weird, I admit.

I sort of stumbled into my John Adams fixation by accident. I was in an American history class that was part joke, part study hall period supervised by the school drama teacher. Anyhow, Mrs. Warner showed us an American Revolution musical called *1776,* so it would look like we were learning. I wasn't exactly impressed. I mean Abigail and John

Adams kept singing these long-distance, heart-to-heart songs that were both boring and lame. What I did like, however, was that everyone in the film hated John Adams. They kept singing that he was too disagreeable to write the Declaration of Independence.

I guess there was something about the collective antipathy toward John Adams that stuck with me. I'm not exactly sure what it was since I wasn't really disliked at the middle school. In fact, people didn't seem to form any opinion of me. They labeled me as the smart girl who reads and acts, and basically let me go relatively unscathed. Maybe what drew me to John Adams was that he seemed to speak his mind. If he didn't like you, he wouldn't go around to everyone else whispering that your wig was out of style or whatever. Oh no, he would go right up to you and air his grievances. That's how I pictured him anyway.

I probably wouldn't have bothered to do the research and find out just how cool he was if it hadn't been for my grandparents on my mom's side. They had a tradition of taking each grandchild on a special trip when they turned thirteen. There were only a few rules:

1. The destination had to be in the United States.

2. It had to be somewhere relatively hassle-free.

3. It had to be educational.

Jordan had gone to Washington, D.C. to see the White House, Jonathan went spelunking in Kentucky, and Shayna had chosen Philadelphia. My first impulse was to pick New York City. I was starting to think of myself as an actress and that it was time I experienced the mecca of the theater world: Broadway. I figured we'd see a few plays, check out some museums, and soak in some history at the same time. However, that trip wasn't to be since, in the wake of September 11th, the stress of security would be too much for my grandpa. So it was up to me to find an alternative.

I was in this state of indecision when John Adams came strolling into my life. I began thinking about the hated president, and then I started researching him. I quickly realized that what I wanted to see was his house in Massachusetts. I wanted to see everything: where he ate, where he sat, where he died. I would have been fine devoting the whole trip to John Adams. Instead, though, I decided I wanted to retrace American history around Boston and beyond. My grandparents agreed, and I threw everything I had into my research—which is how John Adams became my favorite president and did something to me that hadn't happened since fifth grade: made me feel like I was learning. I was going through books on his presidency like some people go through M&M's.

Yes, I was a little strange. Not many kids flip out over John Adams, which was part of my problem. Nobody at the middle school wanted to be there. Not that I blamed them, since I didn't either. It's hard to look forward to long drab corridors and English classes where you don't write and you hardly ever read a book. It was even harder to be excited about the place on a social level. Everyone ran around making others feel lousy, all the while searching for their own identity. It was a mess and it sucked all the life and creativity out of me. So when a real mystery man (John Adams) waltzed into my mind and got me interested again, I refused to go back to my old way of life. I didn't want to spend another year and a half in a perpetual state of boredom.

I knew dropping out of middle school would be a tough sell, so I approached my mom as professionally as possible. After securing her undivided attention, we proceeded to discuss my educational needs. I was painfully thorough and pointed out all the failings in my classes. I knew it wasn't enough though—I had to provide a viable alternative to the problem too. Luckily, I had one. I declared I could home-school just like Natasha. My breathing ceased until she consented to let me switch. I was shocked. I had anticipated her to reply, "Well I know you hate it, honey, but that's life. Only a year and a half left before high school," but she didn't. She gave me a big hug, and said we would find a way to make homeschooling work.

I never regretted making the change. There were a lot of things that needed to be altered and adjusted in my life, and I was finally doing something about it. I was sick and tired of feeling like I had a big sign on me that said "nerd." Like Natasha, I could be anyone I wanted. A fresh start somewhere of my own, somewhere my siblings had never gone, sounded too good to be true. I hadn't been able to figure out who I was in middle school, but I felt like nothing could stop me now. I was ready and eager for a change . . . and I was never to be the same again.

Chapter II

WHEN MY MOM AGREED to let me homeschool, we both knew she wouldn't be my teacher. I don't think we ever really considered it. She despised math, didn't understand science, and had neither the materials nor the time to teach history or English. In the face of all these obstacles, we came up with an excellent solution. I would go to Willow Wind, a homeschooling center not far from my house, for most sub-jects, and learn American history from my aunt.

It felt like everything I wanted was coming true. I had my chance to start over and completely reinvent myself. No longer regarded as the shy bookish girl with no friends, I became the instigator of excitement. I was outgoing and friendly and instantly had a tight-knit group of friends. Part of me couldn't help being surprised that my new friends liked me. At the middle school, drop-dead beautiful girls like Genevieve ("Vieve" was willowy, had long, flowing blond hair, and deep blue eyes—your basic Gwyneth Paltrow look-alike) did not occupy the same social circle as me. They also weren't as genuinely sweet as Vieve . . . they weren't anywhere close. Suddenly, I was hanging out with kids who were smart, cool, beautiful, talented, and who appreciated my company. Did it get any better than that? Surprisingly, yes.

Natasha and I had stayed best friends, and, since she went to Willow Wind too, we were constantly together. We had the same classes, went to concerts, shopped, had sleepovers . . . we were inseparable, and I thought I'd never feel lonely again. My life was a Disney Channel movie, and I wanted it to last forever. Natasha and I even had our own book club. Since we were both romantics and nerds, we read *Pride and Prejudice* before throwing a themed party for two. It began with the five-hour BBC movie version, and continued with breaks for tea, talk, and croquet. I thought if that was what life was like in England, the two of us should hop on the nearest plane to London, since we probably had been born in the wrong country (and possibly the wrong century).

I thought of Natasha, Vieve, and myself as the Unstoppable Trio. We were careful not to exclude anyone at Willow Wind, but at the end of the day it was the two of them I was calling on the phone. I had guy friends at Willow Wind too—a major improvement since my awkwardness had prevented this in the past. The boys at Willow Wind were so different that I didn't worry much about what they thought of me. My friend Eli played the bagpipes, occasionally wore a kilt, was in my tap dancing class, and always spoke his mind. Dash was lanky, tall, gentlemanly, and the perfect candidate for a modern-day knight. To me, they were pretty much perfect.

It wasn't just my social life that changed. I was getting a college-level education. Dash's mom taught the Great Books class where we read everything from *The Aeneid* and Dante's *Inferno* to Chinese poetry. In-class discussions were intense, since everyone did the readings and criticized even the most acclaimed works of literature.

Eli's mom taught a fantastic Philosophy and Religions class that was the highlight of everyone's week. I don't know how someone could not have loved it. For almost two hours a week we became eccentric mini-philosophers. When we discussed the Sufis, everyone learned how to be a whirling dervish while Rumi's poetry was read aloud. We wore sheets as togas and answered questions about Greek and Roman deities before chowing down on a platter of Greek food. I was learning, and best of all, no one ever yelled *BUM-MMM-ER!* at me when

I was confused. School had become my haven. I never wanted to leave again.

Dating, however, messes everything up. Seriously, the safest way to maintain the status quo is to prohibit people from falling in love (or lust), which, I am aware, is impossible to do. Still, if there was a potion that would prevent crushes, I might have administered a few doses in a backwards *A Midsummer Night's Dream* sort of way.

My friends never saw it coming, and frankly neither did I. When, at my Passover seder, Eli's mom mentioned the possibility of a member of the Unstoppable Trio dating Eli, the three of us paused only to trade incredulous looks before saying, "Yeah, he's great, but that's *never* going to happen." If only that had been true.

Natasha was the first one to change her mind. This came as a surprise to me, since she already had a love interest in the form of a boyfriend. Mikhail had been hovering around her in middle school since the first week of *Oliver!* I predicted they'd become the drama club's cutest couple and did my best to assist the inevitable. Mainly, my job was telling Natasha that *of course* Mikhail liked her in a girlfriend kind of way. It took longer than I expected for them to start dating, but they were every bit as adorable as I had anticipated, and it had looked like a smooth relationship to me. Soon after, Natasha got to act in another rendition of *Oliver!* with both her boyfriend and Eli. It wasn't a problem that Mikhail became Eli's friend too. In fact, it was great. Everything was fine. Until it wasn't.

I guess I can't blame anyone for what happened. It wasn't Natasha's fault she had this I'm-super-smart-yet-delicate thing going for her which boys seemed drawn to. Still, when she broke up with her boyfriend and began dating Eli, I didn't handle it very well. I fully realize it was none of my business who Natasha dated, but I didn't want to see Eli get hurt. I also wanted to avoid what would happen when the inevitable rupture occurred. Battle lines would be drawn, and Team Natasha would be facing off against Team Eli. I knew which side I was supposed to be on. She was my best friend, while I still had to look up Eli's phone number before dialing. My loyalty shouldn't have been in question, which is why it really sucked that I knew I was going to side with Eli, mostly because I didn't think Natasha really cared for him, and to me that was a huge deal. Maybe I was being something of a prude, but I just didn't think it was right to yank a guy around if you weren't really interested. Especially if it might destroy a friendship.

On top of that, I was mad at Natasha and had no idea how to express it. I couldn't find the right words. What had happened between us? We had gone from being best friends to playing the roles of the popular one and her trusty side-kick. It was like we were in our own chick flick, and she had just cast me as the nerdy, pathetic friend who is useful only because she boosts the leading lady's self-esteem. If it were *Pride and Prejudice,* she was now Elizabeth Bennet (witty, skinny, instant guy-magnet) and I was Charlotte Lucas (smart but plain, and willing to settle for the most boring and obnoxious guy ever). And I didn't want to be Charlotte. Even more than that, I didn't want to be treated like Charlotte. I thought that best friends should believe they both had leading lady potential. I could have been mistaken, but Natasha didn't seem to see it that way. So I was mad at her, and the Eli situation just made everything worse.

Suddenly, life at Willow Wind began moving in a down-ward spiral, although admittedly, Natasha dating Eli wasn't the total disaster I expected. Their eventual breakup seemed fairly amicable, which is more than I can say for the disinte-gration of our friendship. At some point when I wasn't look-ing, the two of us had morphed into less-than-friends. Something shifted, and suddenly Natasha and I were locked into a twisted competition to prove our status as protago-nists. We went from equals to rivals, and Natasha was defi-nitely the stronger competitor.

When I was at Willow Wind, I thought I was popular; I was pretty universally liked, so I guess I was. A lot of it though, came from being Natasha's friend. And what Natasha giveth, Natasha can taketh away. Our actual disagreement was so small that I figured we could handle it. I told her I was afraid she was just toying with Eli, and that it was important to me she didn't hurt him. She nodded and seemed to understand perfectly. Our underlying issue was still there, but things seemed to be looking up. I didn't think she would call all our friends at Willow Wind to complain about me. Maybe *complain* isn't the right word, but I'm not entirely sure what is. All I know is that suddenly everyone was under the impression I had done something to Natasha along the lines of stabbing her in the back. Nothing could have been further from the truth.

I was suddenly persona non grata. Sure, Vieve, Dash, and Eli were still friendly toward me, but it wasn't the same. Natasha was clearly the queen bee, and I was a drone who had stepped out of place, which didn't exactly help with my low self-esteem issues. Maybe I was being paranoid, but it sure felt like we had disintegrated into an episode of *Gossip Girl*. Vieve and Dash dated, broke up, and muddled the waters even more. Dash was jealous of Eli: Eli was an object of affection, and the girls who liked him worked hard for attention.

It was a mess that killed my love of theater. With the exception of Dash, everyone involved was an actor with a flair for the dramatic. That's when I learned I wanted my drama to stay on the screen or stage. I didn't want to deal with all of it on a daily basis at my school. What I didn't know was that my life was growing increasingly dramatic— and in a way no one had control over, least of all me.

READER/CUSTOMER CARE SURVEY

LTW

We care about your opinions! Please take a moment to fill our online Reader Survey at **http://survey.hcibooks.com**. As a **"THANK YOU"** you will receive a **VALUABLE INSTANT COUPON** towards future book purchases as well as a **SPECIAL GIFT** available only online! Or, you may mail this card back to us to receive **SPECIAL OFFERS!**

First Name		MI.	Last Name	

Address			City	

State		Zip	Email	

1. Gender
☐ Female ☐ Male

2. Age
☐ 11 or younger ☐ 16-19
☐ 12-15 ☐ 24-30
☐ 20-23
☐ 31+

3. Did you receive this book as a gift?
☐ Yes ☐ No

4. What attracts you most to a book?
(Please choose ONE)
___ Title
___ Cover Design
___ Author
___ Subject/Topic

5. How did you find out about this book?
(Please choose ONE)
___ Friend
___ School *(Teacher, Library, etc)*
___ Parent
___ Store Display
___ Interview/Review *(TV, Radio, Print)*
___ Website?

6. Where do you usually buy books?
(Please select your top TWO choices)
___ Bookstore
___ Price Club
___ Retail Store
___ www._____

Comments _____

8. Do you prefer to read books written by:
(Please choose ONE)
___ Teen Authors?
___ Adult Authors?
___ Celebrity
___ No preference

NO POSTAGE
NECESSARY
IF MAILED
IN THE
UNITED STATES

BUSINESS REPLY MAIL

FIRST-CLASS MAIL PERMIT NO 45 DEERFIELD BEACH, FL

POSTAGE WILL BE PAID BY ADDRESSEE

Health Communications, Inc.
3201 SW 15th Street
Deerfield Beach FL 33442-9875

Chapter 12

HOW I GOT THE NOTION that pulling would make things better is a little complicated. For the record: it wasn't Shayna's fault. She only acted as one of the catalysts for my problem. All the decisions I've made are my own—and I've made plenty of wrong ones. To explain, I need to go back to when I was standing by the rabbit hole, and she pointed out the entrance to me.

Shayna was always critiquing my appearance, probably because it made her feel better about her own. She pointed out my pudgy stomach and recommended exercise and a life sentence of no drumsticks. She was right, but I didn't want to hear it, especially since my family had bugged me about my weight for years. My weight came up in conversation whenever I visited my relatives in California, especially when

I saw my Aunt Mirta, a size zero who enjoyed shopping at expensive boutiques. Buying clothes with Mirta was incredibly effective at destroying all my self-confidence in one blow.

So, I had some body image problems, which might explain why I wanted to emulate my skinny friends like Vieve and Natasha. I could never really lose weight, mainly because I got too much enjoyment out of food to restrict myself. I'm fortunate that I only obsessed about my weight and didn't sink into anorexia or bulimia. I wonder if it was just sheer luck that I didn't.

When Shayna critiqued my various body parts, especially my stomach, her words always reverberated around my head until some action was taken to drive them out. Shayna was the first person to tell me I needed to shave my legs. It wasn't a suggestion, like "Well, maybe you should consider . . ." According to her, it was a necessity since I resembled a monkey. So, I took a fresh razor from my mom and performed that rite of passage.

Unfortunately, not all of Shayna's beauty demands were that simple. In fact, her next one was that I tweeze my eyebrows. She told me I had a unibrow. I tried to shrug off her comment, but she kept scrunching up her face and repeating it. I didn't know what to think or how to grade eyebrows. In my mind, they were just sort of there to be ignored. I thought mine were okay, but I couldn't get the word out of my head and heard a persistent chant of, "Unibrow, unibrow, unibrow," relentlessly pounding into my brain. I honestly didn't even know what it meant, but I could tell it wasn't good. I began to pull.

It was harmless at first. Nothing could have been more innocent, albeit misguided. I pinched my nails together (or what little there was since I had a nail-biting habit too) and attacked my eyebrows. When I started I hadn't heard of tweezers. Well, I had, but only in terms of removing splinters. I had no idea that anyone would ever use the tool to select what hairs they wanted to remove. Somehow, I had made it to eighth grade without ever considering how people got perfectly shaped eyebrows, which was easily accomplished because I had never looked at eyebrows before. I didn't know that tweezing was supposed to be precise. I just focused my attention on the task ahead of me and pulled. I tugged on my eyebrows wherever my fingers closed around hair. I was sure I was doing a good thing, something to make me prettier. I thought maybe boys might notice me, but it didn't work out the way I'd hoped.

I had no idea what I was doing. I knew that, but I couldn't bring myself to ask anyone for help. I had asked my mom once before about unibrows and she had sort of dismissed the question. I had too little self-confidence to even try to find the answer in an issue of *Seventeen* magazine. They always had skinny, fashionably dressed teenagers on the cover, which only made me feel more uncomfortable with my appearance when I so much as glanced at them. The last thing I wanted to do was discuss my physical flaws with Shayna, so she was out of the running too. That left me with Natasha and Vieve. In hindsight, I could have asked them. I'm almost positive that I should have asked them . . . just started the conversation one day with, "Hey, so do you guys know what a unibrow is? Because I have no idea." But they were both so beautiful, I couldn't bring myself to do it.

I decided to get my eyebrows "under control" before mentioning it to anyone. So, when I was alone, I pulled at them. It hurt. No big surprise, right? I was yanking out my eyebrows with my fingers—*of course* it hurt. The thing that struck me as weird wasn't the pain, or even that I kept pulling through the pain, but that after a while there was no pain. That's the part most people don't know because they don't do it long enough to find out. The immediate stab of pain and the muffled "Ouch!" that accompanied my pulling would soon give way to a pleasurable feeling. Pulling made me feel fantastic! Even though the area where I pulled turned a tomato shade of red, the whole thing was both relaxing and exhilarating. It was sort of like a fireworks display: it played with my senses, turned off my brain, and left me longing for the next burst of activity. I didn't realize that until it was way too late. I was hooked before I knew I had begun.

The details of my new habit may seem disturbing. They disturb me, and I'm the one who did it. The truth is, in many ways, pulling is like cracking knuckles or wiggling a loose tooth. It's refreshing in a shot-of-caffeine-to-the-system sort of way. It felt natural. What could be so wrong with pulling when it perked me up and made me feel alive? I sure didn't know the answer to that question, and I wasn't inclined to look into it deeply. The pulling felt so good that I couldn't stop. I really didn't want to quit even if I could.

I think what I loved the most about pulling was that, while I was doing it, I wasn't thinking. I've always been the sort of person who sees a simple situation and begins analyzing it to death. I searched for hidden meanings in everything (and am now left wondering whether that is responsible for the loss of several friendships).

I didn't only overthink my own life, either. I stayed up late at night listening to conversations between characters in the latest book I had read. Not because I wanted to have them in my head, but because I couldn't get them out. To make matters worse, the conversations weren't even in the books.

I couldn't just read something and set it aside. The characters would go on past the happily-ever-afters and have adventures in my mind. This might have been fun if it weren't so intrusive. What I wanted was to sleep, not to be the third wheel in my own brain! For a while I listened to the same book on tape every night until I had it memorized, just in the hope that if I knew it well I'd be able to sleep. The only thing that happened was I could soon quote *The Twinkie Squad,* a feat that impressed nobody.

Pulling was far more effective at turning off my brain. It let me zone out. I sort of went into a pulling trance. The real world would slip away, and when I refocused it was to find a pile of hair in front of me, which, while not exactly the nicest way to come back to Earth, wasn't the worst either—or so I thought at the time.

I didn't set out to hurt myself when I started pulling (unless it was on some subconscious level). I honestly thought it was good for me. So good that I began using it as a reward system. When I was bored with my homework but did it anyway, I got to pull. Sometimes I even used pulling as a motivation to keep working. I loved everything about it: the way my fingers clenched and tensed, the sound a hair made as it was removed from my eyebrow (so quiet you could hardly hear it), the moist tip of the hair that felt so cool in the palm of my hand. It was satisfying and yet always left me wanting more. I required the sensation, craved it even, and my body had no choice but to give me what I demanded. So, I pulled and listened and played with the hairs. It became a habit. I took solace in my pulling and used it to escape the world around me. That's why I continued doing it long after I should have stopped.

My mom was the first person to notice I had gone too far . . . or at least the first person to comment on it. I realized I had a problem only a few weeks before she did. My eyebrows were becoming perilously thin, and I was getting the distinct impression it was not an attractive look. I couldn't seem to stop though. It felt so natural. I couldn't quite believe how the action had become a habit in the space of a few weeks, but that didn't change the facts. Fact: My eyebrows had dwindled to the point of nonexistence. Fact: I loved pulling, and I never wanted to stop. Fact: I had to figure out a way to stop.

All the facts in the world wouldn't have made it easier for me to stop, though. Especially since I wasn't sure I really had a problem. I knew the state of my eyebrows needed to be fixed, but I figured that didn't necessarily mean there was something wrong with me.

When I couldn't figure out a way to help myself, my mom intervened. She gently asked me what was going on. Of course, by the time she had worked up the nerve to confront me, my eyebrows were even thinner. I barely had a line of hair over each eye. I knew it looked bad. I knew it, but I still couldn't bring myself to stop. I didn't tell my mom the whole story. I left out the part about how pulling made me feel alive and relaxed and happy and how I didn't really want to stop. I didn't think it would change the situation—and I was probably right. I either had to stop pulling or show up for my first day at Ashland High School without eyebrows. That prospect sounded almost as bad to me as going to school naked. Maybe worse, since in my case there was no waking up from the nightmare.

My mom warned ominously that unless it ended, I would resemble an elderly woman with makeup pencil lines where my eyebrows should have been. The image of a hairless existence has haunted me ever since. That I might have to try one of those hair-growth products they advertise for bald people on late-night television terrified me. I couldn't look at people's faces the same way anymore. I fixated on eyebrows, examining the shape and degree of bushiness, all the while praying they weren't reciprocating. Whenever I spotted what I termed "unnecessary hairs" on other people, I longed to pluck them. I actually fantasized about taking a pair of tweezers to strangers, to friends, to relatives.

I was sure I had gone off the deep end. My urges led me to use tweezers so I could be more precise in my tweezing. That didn't mean I had control over the pulling. My brother Jonathan kept looking at me quizzically and asking what was different. He couldn't put his finger on what had changed, but even he knew something wasn't how it used to be. I just shrugged my shoulders and hoped with all my might that no one would be able to figure it out. Once I was hooked, my time was spent in an anxious, terrified state as I tried to hide my pulling from the world. The more I thought about people finding out, the worse I felt. My stomach wriggled, and my heart sped up. The only thing that calmed me down was to pull, which only made the problem worse.

Somehow, I managed to stifle my urge the summer before high school. I don't know how, and I really wish I did. If I were to guess, it was because the prospect of being considered a freak in high school scared me to the point of immobility. I also think it was because at that time, I didn't know how to hide my condition. The only trick in my arsenal was eyebrow pencil, and I swore to myself that I would never use it ever again. I knew using the pencil made me look better than having nothing there, but the idea of being dependent upon it for the rest of my life almost made me break out into a cold sweat.

For a month and a half, I was able to stay pretty much clean. Much to my relief, my eyebrows grew back, and I began high school with no one aware of my condition. I just wondered how I was going to survive without friends.

Chapter 13

HIGH SCHOOL IS INFINITELY better than middle school. By ninth grade, most kids are done being cruel to others just to make themselves feel better. Another improvement is the fact that high school actually matters. Colleges check high school transcripts, so being smart and working hard actually pays off. Getting out of high school and into a good university was enough to motivate most of my classmates to study. It was more than enough to ensure I kept hitting the books. Frankly, I didn't care about high school, but I knew all along that college was my end game.

College was my version of Neverland, except instead of staying a kid, I would live the life I'd imagined for myself. College was where I would calmly sip coffee while discussing obtuse philosophical theories. College was where I was supposed to become cool and collected and put together. All I had to do was survive four years of public schooling (I was done with Willow Wind), and I would be on my way.

So, I was very careful and deliberate in creating my high school plan, penciling in four years of French, science, math, and other important subjects. With Shayna's help, I planned a schedule that showed I was both well-balanced and studious. What it actually proved, though, was that I was overly ambitious.

Biology was way over my head. As one of two freshmen to land in the class, I sat mutely in a room filled with intimidating sophomores and juniors, and tried to understand why I should care about mitosis. (My answer: I shouldn't.) My complete lack of interest in the subject left me scrambling for a way to pick up my grade. I scurried over to the library and read the extra credit books about disease and destruction just to stay in the B range. I didn't enjoy the books, but the worst part of the extra credit deal was the inquisition style, one-on-one book report with Mr. M. afterwards.

"So, Marni," he slowly drawled after class. "What's *The Hot Zone* about?"

I was fully prepared.

"Well, there is a disease that's spreading, and it makes people *hemorrhage* and die."

Maybe if I had been a science person, I would have known that hemorrhage is pronounced "hem-ridge" not "hem-or-hodge." Instead, I was an English-and-American-history kind of girl with a tendency to mispronounce things.

Mr. M. looked completely mystified, which only made me babble longer. It also led me to misuse the word *hemorrhage* about a hundred times more.

"Um . . . yeah," I dribbled out finally.

"Marni," said Mr. M., "what is a hem-or-hodge?"

In my nervous state I relied on a sudden burst of hand gestures to get my point across.

"You know, when someone is bleeding out. Hemorrhage."

It was like a painful game of charades with me wildly motioning blood spurting from my arteries. That afternoon it became clear we didn't speak the same language, and that when it came to science, I would always be in the wrong.

My luck didn't improve in French class. The endless verb conjugations, the masculine and feminine words, and the snooty accent all evaded me. I would sit in a state of confusion thinking, *"Merde, merde, merde!"* ("Shit, shit, shit!"), while the perky popular girls chatted away Parisian-style. I dreaded the class, especially when we were dealing with numbers.

The French go out of their way to destroy American brains with their number system. For example, instead of just saying ninety-three in a straightforward manner, they have to say four times twenty plus thirteen. As if this isn't confusing at all. *Not.*

It was the number game (also known as the public humiliation game) that really got to me. The teacher would pass out cards with two numbers on them. In English, it would go like this:

ME: I have 45. Who has 78?
OTHER CLASSMATE: I have 78. Who has 27?

Simple, right? The problem was that I couldn't pronounce my numbers in French or even figure them out for that matter. I only knew my card was being called because everyone groaned and searched for the blockhead who wasn't speaking up. Did I mention that the whole thing was timed? The popular girls would roll their eyes in exasperation, and when it was discovered I was the weak link, things only got worse. They'd march up to me after class and demand to know why I couldn't get it right. I thought it was fairly obvious: I sucked at French and was even worse at math.

Math class was straight-up boring. At Willow Wind, I had a free tutor with a sense of humor. Getting used to a classroom setting after that was a hard adjustment. I had no idea what we were doing in class and struggled to keep my eyes open. I ended up copying most of my homework from the back of the book. Yes, technically this is cheating, but since I wasn't learning, I doubted my education was being compromised. That's how I rationalized it anyway.

I doubt I would have passed any of my math classes if it hadn't been for Gwyn. Our reconciliation couldn't have happened at a better time. Since the two of us lived on the same street, we had seen each other from time to time throughout middle school (and in my case Willow Wind). It was always very friendly. We chatted a little if we passed ways, and we said hi in the grocery store. Still, ever since I had my flash that Gwyn didn't really care about me, I had steered clear. As Gwyn later put it (and I agree), I was being an idiot.

During high school, we both walked down our hill to the high school at the same time, and we fell into our old pattern of talking. At first, it felt awkward. I had no idea what to say. "Hey, how has life been treating you since we parted ways at the end of elementary school?" The conversation flowed naturally though, partly because Gwyn hadn't really changed. She was still short, sarcastic, methodical, and absolutely wonderful. It wasn't long before I was back to my old routine of stopping at her house every day after school. Since no one in her family had an aversion to cooking (unlike me and my mom), her refrigerator was always stocked with delicious-ness. The two of us would make nachos, listen to music, and hang out, while she explained math to me. With a cheese-laden chip in hand, I learned a billion times more math from Gwyn than I ever did from any teacher.

The best part about reuniting with Gwyn, though, was that I got my best friend back. There was no drama with Gwyn, she never said one thing and did another. She was very up front—what you see is what you get. Life with Gwyn made everything better.

However, even Gwyn couldn't save me from freshman health, which was probably the class where I was the fur-thest behind. I didn't know the first thing about drugs and had only tasted alcohol once at my bat mitzvah, when unbe-knownst to me, the rabbi put wine in my glass instead of grape juice. Everyone else in my class knew about uppers and downers and that *DUI* didn't stand for "Dolphin Under Interrogation." They knew about sex and drugs (and prob-ably rock and roll), while I was clueless. I didn't feel like I could really ask either, especially not about sex. Even though I didn't know the answer, I couldn't imagine inquiring, "Yeah, so is it true that, um . . . a certain part of the male anatomy goes . . . up?" I decided it was time to get some answers from a source I could trust. So, I turned to Chris.

The only reason I knew a boy I could ask for advice was because we had met on a cruise I had gone on with my grandparents. It was a great trip, as I could spend all day seeing various ports in Europe, and spend my nights as far away from Shayna as possible. In order to meet some new people, I went to the teen club and was fortunate enough to find Chris and Josh. They were both thin boys with dark brown hair, but that was where the similarities ended. Chris was prone to swearing and wanted to have a convincing Canadian accent. Josh, on the other hand, was superpolite and only revealed his authentic Canadian accent once he heard Chris butchering it. With my mom's permission, I found myself wandering the ship with them until two in the morning. The knowledge that I'd probably never see them again was incredibly liberating. We shared our pasts, danced, joked around, drank tea at midnight, and ran around the ship until the three of us were officially friends. On the last night of the trip, we all exchanged e-mail addresses and promised to write. I never imagined I would remain in contact with both of them. This came in handy in many ways—not least of all for my health class.

Chris was a high school senior in New York, and I felt cool simply by association. I asked him all my embarrassing questions for some insight into the male psyche. The information he provided me with was more than a little terrifying. My mouth dropped open as I read his e-mails and I would burst out into laughter with my face flushed red with embarrassment. Chris also offered me some horrendous advice. He said that if I really wanted a boyfriend, I should just grab a guy, pull him into a bathroom, and start making out. There were so many problems with this idea, I didn't know where to begin.

For starters, there was no way I could have pulled it off. At the very least, I would have tripped and crashed into a sink or ended up on the floor. Plus, if I had the nerve to grab a guy (which I didn't), they would probably want to know what the hell I was doing. To which I would wittily reply "Um . . ." Somehow, I doubted my bumbling attempts at seduction would result in my having a boyfriend. I also knew I didn't want my first kiss to be in a bathroom with someone flushing a few stalls away. Not exactly romantic.

So instead of taking advice from Chris, I listened to Josh. Josh lived in Canada, played hockey in his free time, and told me to just be myself. Not surprisingly, I decided to go with that and concentrate on surviving high school without the status of a social pariah. It wasn't as hard as I thought. The popular kids ignored me, but once again I found my niche. I was lucky enough to find some genuinely nice kids who were painfully straightlaced and exceptionally largehearted. My friends were band geeks and science nerds who shared my love of classic oldies and puns. None of us were particularly wild, not that we had much of an opportunity since we usually spent our weekends doing homework. We didn't party, drink, or break rules, which doesn't mean we were boring—just tame. Around them, I could do anything, including singing at the top of my lungs in a British accent during lunch and sweet-talking the cafeteria ladies into free muffins. There were perks that came with my "good girl" image and my solitary dimple.

I regained my footing slowly as I created new friends and reconnected with old ones. Still, my freshman year at Ashland High School was rough. The fact that Shayna was there didn't make it any easier. Having an older sister should have come with benefits. It didn't. It just made my status as a pathetic little freshman all the more obvious. Shayna had a reputation as being one of the smartest girls in the school, which added pressure on me to measure up. She was also a princess, literally. She applied for a scholarship, and the next thing we knew she was taking princess lessons and preparing for the Oregon title of Pear Blossom Princess. Despite the fact that this was as lame as it sounds and that she came in third place, she still received money for college and got to wear a tiara. Trust me—it's not easy being the younger sibling of a royal.

It didn't matter how invisible I tried to be: recognition was impossible to avoid. People kept asking if I knew my sister was running for Pear Blossom Princess. I always replied politely that I did and wondered how they thought I could've missed that detail. According to Shayna, a lot of people mentioned me to her and what they had to say wasn't exactly complimentary.

At school, we maintained a sort of truce. It was considered sacred ground and came with its own set of rules for how we would interact. These included:

1. No conversation.
2. Limited eye contact.
3. No participation or membership in any of her clubs/ activities.
4. Limited conversations with her friends.
5. No existence allowed except an invisible one.

These rules, of course, were only for my benefit. If I followed them to the letter, she was less likely to scream at me in private. I followed them exactly and walked a respectful fifteen feet behind her on our way to school. I scurried past her in the hallways and scuttled out of my English/global studies class as she entered for AP world history.

We both tried diligently to avoid each other and be associated with our brothers. It didn't matter that Shayna and I used different last names—we were both lumped together. Shayna used her Hebrew middle name, while I signed everything with my mom's maiden name. It didn't stop teachers from comparing us to each other. Since she was so quick-witted and sharp, I was certain any comparison between us did not bode well for me.

That wasn't the only problem lurking in wait.

Chapter 14

IT STARTED OUT MUCH AS it had before—a quick tug at my eyebrows every now and again and everything seemed better. I've heard stories that sometimes in dangerous situations when the adrenaline is flowing and whatnot, people become hyperaware of their surroundings. Hair pulling isn't like that. I didn't become more aware . . . rather, I became more awake. I pulled and felt better, which was always followed by regret. I would look at my face and ask why I was so set on destroying it.

Pulling became my addiction—my personal heroin. Hair-oine. But just because I was hooked didn't mean I was careless. I'd learned several lessons from the first time I had pulled, the most firmly entrenched was the importance of discretion. If no one knew you were pulling, then no one would be able to comment on it. No one would warn against a future that involved tattooed or penciled-on eyebrows. I knew I had to be secretive, or I would be discovered. So I diversified.

Eyelashes have a completely different feel to them. The gesture is the same, but the sensation is even more enjoyable. The perfect tug gets a simultaneous popping sound as the eyelash is removed and the eyelid adheres to the eye. It became the newest branch of my obsession, but it wasn't enough. I needed something else to be effective. So, I began pulling my hair. First it was the back of my head, then above my forehead, and finally behind my ears. As soon as one spot was demolished, I moved on to another. It was sort of like deforestation. I was clear-cutting my hair in one area before abandoning it for untouched locations. I wasn't proud of myself, but I couldn't stop.

Abraham Lincoln once said, "You may fool all the people some of the time; you can even fool some of the people all the time; but you can't fool all of the people all the time." He was dead-on. Not that I didn't have a plan. When I pulled from the top of my head, I knew I had to wear a baseball cap for a month, so no one would think I was balding. When I pulled out my eyebrows, I had to position my bangs so that the eyebrows themselves were barely visible. When I pulled out my bangs, I had to lop off some of my hair to get more bangs to hide what I had done. Hats and scarves helped hide the pulling behind my ears, and I wore them daily.

I was also careful about when I pulled. I couldn't get away with doing it in conversation, but in class I would assess the risk factor, and, if I didn't think anyone was looking, I would tug. Pulling behind the ear was the easiest to hide in the presence of others. It looked like I was just toying with my hair, not that I was yanking it out one piece at a time.

The best time to pull was during tests. Everyone was so focused on the paper in front of them that no one noticed if I was methodically yanking out my bangs. Tests were also the times I felt the need to pull the most; I pulled to relax, and consequently whenever I was stressed or sleep-deprived, my urge became even more pronounced. I remember taking a chemistry exam my senior year, and, even though I had been so proud of the way my bangs were growing back in, in the course of that one test all my hard work was undone. I left the science room a few hours later hoping the janitors wouldn't notice that 2 percent of my hair was on the floor surrounding my desk instead of on my scalp. I tried to prevent anyone from noticing by surreptitiously spreading the hair around a bit and throwing some of it away in the trash. Sometimes I had no choice but to roll my hair up in a ball and stick it in a sweatshirt pocket for later disposal. At the end of the day, I often had huge hairballs that I would stare at in amazement, wondering how all that hair could've been attached to my head that morning and ripped out by late afternoon.

Despite my best efforts to pull discreetly, I wasn't fooling everybody. In fact, I wasn't fooling anybody. Most of my classmates must have known there was *something* going on, but they didn't want to say anything to my face. Part of the reason was probably because they had no idea what was actually wrong with me. If I had been throwing up in the bathroom stall after lunch every day, I'm sure someone would have reported me to the school psychiatrist so I could get help for bulimia. I suspect that since no one knew what to make of my pulling, they just did nothing. I much preferred that to the alternative.

The first person to give me a hard time about my eyebrows (or lack thereof) was Simona. She was one of those girls you couldn't help taking an instant dislike to, or at least, I couldn't. She had a way of speaking that made it clear to whomever she was addressing that they were infinitely inferior. I never was one to appreciate that. Nor did I like having her repeatedly approach me during our English/global studies class and ask me in her squeaky, high-pitched voice what happened to my eyebrows.

I never knew what to say. "Sorry, I have this compulsion to rip my hair out. And how was your weekend?" I doubted *that* would go over well. I knew how I wanted to reply. I wanted to look her in the eye and answer earnestly, "They got caught in a blender." I tried to picture her expression. Shock? Confusion? Disdain? I wasn't sure what her reaction would be, but I knew I could never say it. If I had mentioned a blender (or any other household appliance) or admitted I had a problem, it would have spread everywhere. I really didn't want to be the girl with a "problem" who had everybody whispering. It would be only a small step from that to meetings with the school counselors. I had left therapy behind me when I entered Willow Wind, and I was in no rush to return. All I wanted was to fly happily under the radar with my friends on the geek squad.

So I didn't mention any blenders. I didn't say anything. Instead, I pasted a blank expression on my face and pretended to be distracted by some inanimate object in the distance. I would do a double take as if just realizing she was speaking to me before excusing myself to talk to the teacher about my latest essay. Simona never believed my act for a second. She also didn't read it as a clear signal to get lost and never mention my eyebrows again. In fact, she brought it up throughout the year. If Simona's goal was to mortify me, she succeeded beyond her wildest dreams. I considered myself properly humiliated. After an encounter with her, all I felt capable of doing was disappearing into television and books. A trip to the school library was always in order to lighten my mood. At least it was until a librarian decided to pry.

I remember being happy when I crossed the threshold into the library that day. Simona hadn't been bothering me recently, and I thought with pride that my eyebrows were growing back in nicely. It was as I perused the books on display that Mr. S. sidled up to me. Mr. S. had never bothered me before. He wasn't my favorite librarian, but it's hard to compete with Judy, who usually worked the checkout desk and gave me energy bars when I missed lunch. Still, I didn't really mind Mr. S. We'd had a few conversations about books, but that was pretty much it. We certainly weren't close enough for me to tell him a secret—particularly not my deepest, darkest one.

So it was unusual, but not surprising, when Mr. S. walked over to me. I figured he would say, "Hi, Marni, how's your day going?" or "Have you seen this new book?" or something equally neutral. Instead, he asked what happened to my eyelashes. Until then, I hadn't realized it was noticeable. I was so focused on my eyebrows, I wasn't aware that my eyelashes were noticeably sparse. I stared at him blankly, said something like

"I have to go," and fled. It wasn't just the question that had startled me—mostly it was the questioner. I felt indignant. What right did the Mr. S's and the Simonas of the world have to interrogate me? I wasn't their friend. They didn't know me at all. To make matters worse, I was being attacked in the library—my happy place, my haven, my sanctuary . . . my sacred ground. Of course, the question would have hurt no matter where I was standing. It hurt in the classroom, and it hurt in the library, and it hurt in my bedroom, where I played it over and over again in my head. I was stuck in a world of hurt, and the only thing that cleared my head was more pulling. And so the hurting continued.

Chapter 15

I HAPPILY TOOK MY GEEKDOM to a whole new level my freshman year. As soon as I joined speech and debate, I was certain I had found my calling. I was destined to become a debate nerd who would inspire mini–debate nerds for years to come. I loved being a member of the Ashland Speech and Debate team. Part of the appeal was that it never made me feel lame—instead, I felt quite the opposite, since I was taught debate by senior boys who intimidated every freshman within a mile radius into silence. They were incredibly smart and could randomly cite all sorts of philosophic theories to support their arguments. I hoped their coolness might rub off by association.

I marked myself down for four years of speech and debate in my high school plan and did everything I could to become a valued member of the team. I even donated my dad's old suits and an enormous bag of ties from my great-uncle, single-handedly outfitting roughly half of the debate boys. I was completely dedicated until Ms. T. shattered my plans.

Ms. T. was the debate coach who made Simona appear hypersensitive and compassionate in comparison. To be honest, I still haven't come up with an analogy that does her justice—devil incarnate and Cruella de Vil are both missing a certain something. I mean, how do you describe a woman who went out of her way to torture you?

Ms. T.'s animosity towards me was so obvious that everyone on the team knew about it. Nick, a sophomore who, funnily enough, bore an uncanny resemblance to a young Nick Lachey, actually created a game out of her hatred. It was called "Let's Get Marni in Trouble." The object of the game was to see how many times he could get Ms. T. to glare at me. It didn't take much of an effort, since the slightest disturbance in the classroom produced instant death-ray glances. I had to steel myself before entering the class, since I was submitting myself to an hour of intense hatred every time. Things only got worse when she accidentally left me at a Fred Meyer in Forest Grove, Oregon.

The speech and debate team always went to Fred Meyer the night before a tournament. Like Target or Walmart, it was the perfect place to stock up on last-minute debate sup-plies (like pens and legal pads) before the competition. Anyhow, I was dressed up in my suit and heels looking for something to eat from the deli section, when my teammates boarded the bus without conducting a proper head check, which is how I was abandoned in a hick town in the middle of nowhere. I reached the parking lot just in time to see the orange tail lights fade into the night. So there I was at eleven o'clock at night with almost no money, no cell phone, and five hours away from home. To make matters worse, I had just completed an extra credit project in health class (to com-pensate for my low grade on a drug quiz) on rape. I thor-oughly researched the topic and had stared at terrifying statistics on sexual assaults. One situation in particular I was repeatedly warned against: standing alone in dark parking lots at night. So it shouldn't come as a surprise that I began to freak out.

I started quivering uncontrollably and muttering to myself to get a grip. I needed to formulate a plan, but all I could hear was Shayna's voice reverberating in my head from all those years ago, telling me her greatest fear was that someday I would be raped. That night, it became my biggest fear too. I kept my head, though. I thought about *Pride and Prejudice* and asked myself what the heroine, Elizabeth Bennet, would do in my situation. I didn't have the faintest idea, but the question helped keep the panic at bay. When the bus didn't come rumbling back, I decided that if Elizabeth Bennet had access to modern technology in the form of telephones, she would be calling someone for assistance.

I got lucky. By a stroke of fortune, I remembered the name of the hotel the team was staying at and, with the help of a Fred Meyer employee, was patched through to Ms. T. Our conversation was short and began with me blurting out, "You left me!" and Ms. T. asking for the identity of the caller. It took well over a half an hour for the bus to pull into Fred Meyer to stage my rescue. By that point, my body was shaking feverishly and continued to jerk for hours until the adrenaline began to settle into my system. Ms. T. wasn't on the bus to pick me up, and she hadn't asked how I was doing over the phone. *Nice.* I never knew why she disliked me with every fiber of her bony little body, but after awhile, the feeling was mutual.

I'm not sure why abandoning me at Fred Meyer made her hate me more, but it did. Her glances became increasingly contemptuous as time went on. Still, instead of ditching the team at the end of first semester like any normal person would have, I withstood her hatred my entire freshman year because I loved the team. Although admittedly, I did have some other incentives to stay, one of which was the boys.

I was the only freshman girl on the team. This was both astounding and rather uncomfortable. However, I was not the only freshman, not by a long shot. It also just so happened that all the boys I had a crush on were also debating. Despite my continued inability to flirt, a skill I had not even attempted to master, I could still hang out with them. I knew eating pizza together at tournaments didn't exactly make us friends. It just elevated me to good acquaintance status, which was as high as I ever expected to go, since the guys on the team were attractive and popular, and their female counterparts had practically pasted a RESERVED sign on their foreheads in shiny lip gloss.

I did try to flirt once. Well, sort of. I never really got to the flirting part before screwing it up. After school one day, I spotted Graham standing outside a classroom. Graham was one of the nicest boys among the freshmen, possibly among the entire high school population. He had wavy, dark hair and big, brown eyes. Most of the girls I knew would have agreed he was crush-worthy. Mainly though, he was just plain nice, and I never worried that, like Nick, he'd try to get Ms. T. to glare at me.

Anyhow, I saw him standing there looking all nice and adorable, and I impulsively decided to take my friend Chris' advice. Not the grabbing and kissing advice, but the flirting advice. As in: *Just try it*. So I casually walked up to him and said, "Hey, Graham, what's up with you?"

I just wish I had been able to say it . . . not spray it. One second Graham was perfectly dry and cute, and the next, his face was soaked with my saliva. I was horrified. This had *never* happened to me before, and I had no idea what to do. Graham was too nice to comment, but he delicately dabbed at himself and mentioned something about waiting for a friend. I just nodded foolishly and flashed back to a quiz in a girly magazine I had read in the dentist's office about embarrassing situations. There was one question that involved accidental spray-age. I desperately tried to remember what options A, B, and C had been, since the asteroid I was praying for wasn't coming fast enough. I decided the way to go was to act lighthearted about it.

"I guess I really got you there," I said sheepishly. "Sorry about that."

Graham assured me it was fine, and, after a few more minutes of awkwardness, I made a hasty retreat. I promised myself that if I spotted a really big rock on the way home I would curl up into a little ball under it and die.

That probably helps explain why I remained single throughout high school. I'd like to think the real reason was because dating at school seemed kind of gross. People had known each other for so long they were sort of like siblings. However, this is coming from someone who never had a single date, so what do I know? Maybe I'm just trying to rationalize my boyfriendless existence. The truth? I wanted one. Although it's possible I didn't want a boyfriend so much as I wanted to find Mr. Darcy from *Pride and Prejudice*. Unfortunately, he didn't attend Ashland High School (I double-checked). I didn't actually even want to date the guys I had crushes on, which might explain why my interest didn't last long. In my senior year, Graham was telling me how ardently he loved me (technically, it was Lysander telling Helena in Shakespeare's *A Midsummer Night's Dream*, but *still . . .*), and I was completely immune.

Possibly, my pulling was also a factor in my boyfriendless existence. Not because boys were repulsed by my condition (I worked damn hard at hiding it to avoid just that predicament), but because my pulling made it impossible to picture myself dating anyone. In the movies, the guy raises the girl's face up to gaze into before slowly kissing her. I didn't think it would work too well if some guy looked at my face closely pre-kiss and noticed my eyebrows were missing. I also couldn't exactly let a guy romantically push the bangs out of my eyes. If he tried I would surely stiffen up, hold my breath, and hope he didn't notice that underneath that curtain of bangs was a stubble of growth as my old bangs tried desperately to return to their rightful place. My fear of a boyfriend (or potential boyfriend) running away in disgust stopped me from ever trying to flirt. I kept telling myself that once my pulling was under control, I would try to put myself out there. That never happened.

Despite my failure at flirting, the debate boys were still a pretty big incentive to stay on the team. I also really enjoyed debating. I loved that when I held the floor, I could say anything I wanted to persuade people. I was also slowly getting good. It took me a while to get the knack of debating, since Ms. T. had prevented me from debating at the first tournament, but I started winning awards. I was sure if I went to debate camp over the summer, as a sophomore I'd be able to demolish my opponents.

Ms. T. told everyone that debate camp was essential. I had done my research and was prepared to spend my summer talking about utilitarianism, justice, and equality. I decided to look beyond the nonstop hostility, the snide comments, the underhanded insults, and the glaring from Ms. T. to focus on what really mattered—debating. At least, I did until Ms. T. made me stay after class one day so we could have a "little talk" without any witnesses. That was when I learned the true definition of cruel.

"Marni," Ms. T. began, "I don't think you should go to debate camp."

Since she had been declaring the importance of debate camp for well over a month, I was plenty shocked.

I tried to look calm and serene as I replied, "Oh? And why is that?"

"I don't think you're mature enough for it," she said, coldly.

I sat back, flabbergasted. This coming from a woman who had messed up a head count and left me stranded at Fred Meyer. But she was just getting started. Ms. T. went on to inform me that:

1. No one on the team liked me.
2. I wasn't a "good fit."
3. My English/global studies teacher had described me as "pushy" and said I "did not know when to quit."
4. The senior boys didn't like me sitting near them in the back of the bus.
5. I showed a complete lack of respect for the team, its hierarchy, and its traditions.
6. My footwear was inappropriate.

Okay, she might not have called me out for forgetting to wear heels to the first tournament, but I could tell she was thinking about it. And those were just some of the high-lights. By the time she had finished verbally abusing me in every possible manner, the hallways were deserted. I had no idea how long the roast had gone on, but if insults were a way to measure time, I should've been graduating from high school and never looking back.

When I finally left the room and the intense glare of her steely blue eyes, I felt unable to do even the simplest of things, like breathing. I knew walking home wasn't a physical possibility. I'd barely gone a few steps to use the phone before I broke down. I'm still amazed my mom was able to understand what I gargled into the receiver. I was shattered, and my sobbing was uncontrollable.

My mom rushed into action and categorically refused to let me have anything to do with Ms. T. ever again. Leaving the team wasn't enough to make things better though. Telling the school principal the truth—that Ms. T. was an abusive teacher who tortured students and favored the boys—wasn't enough. The sight of wispy blonde curls still scared me. I'd panic at the mere thought of running into her. I even had a nightmare about Ms. T. that summer when I was traveling with my mom and Shayna. Out of nowhere, in the middle of the night, I bolted upright and sobbed in a petrified voice, "Ms. T.!"

My mom patted my shoulders and hugged me and told me it was over. It was all over. One therapist and two years later, I was finally able to start putting speech and debate behind me. Considering it was in speech and debate that I first experienced anti-Semitism (a group of boys from a different team called me "Jew Girl" and told me to "go control the economy"), it's sort of amazing it didn't take even longer. Speech and debate was also where I first told the truth about my eyebrows. There were plenty of reasons I needed therapy to move beyond it.

Chapter 16

I THOUGHT I'D LOST MY MIND. That's what the pulling did to me—it made me question my sanity, which is probably the scariest thing that has ever happened to me. Once I started thinking I had gone insane, I lost the ability to trust myself. After all, everything I was thinking was coming from a madwoman, so why should I listen to anything she had to say? I was splitting myself into first person and third person and wondering if I even was a person and, if so, what kind of a person that was. It certainly wasn't the type of person I wanted to be. My pulling made me despise myself, loathe myself, hold myself in abhorrence . . . the words don't really matter if the sentiment remains the same. Other people's reaction to my missing facial hair stung but didn't come close to the pain and intensity of my self-resentment.

I had no idea what was wrong with me. All I knew was that I wanted to pull, and, according to society, that made me a freak. No one came up to me and said, "If you are ripping your hair out, you should be put into a mental institution," but that's what I thought. No one ever convinced me otherwise. Sure, health class covered anorexia and bulimia, but that was about it. I remember sitting there waiting for someone to mention ripping out hair. I even considered mentioning it casually. I would just ask, "And is hair pulling a common stress disorder too?" But I knew if I did my secret would be revealed. So I kept my mouth shut and extracted meaning from the silence. I thought the absence of conversation on pulling meant it was somehow worse than other disorders. I pictured a whole spectrum of disorders. On one end you had the ones we learned about in class that society could understand, and on the other end you had me. I thought pulling was so wrong it was unspeakable.

I didn't talk about it outside of class, either. No way. If people wanted to know I was mentally unhinged, they could figure it out for themselves. So, I protected my secret and instantly regretted the one time I let my guard down. Instead of confessing to my mom or Gwyn or even Chris or Josh through the privacy of e-mails, I opened up to one of my teammates on the speech and debate team. There were several reasons why I never should have told this particular girl. We weren't friends (I don't even remember her name), she was a high school senior, she had a reputation for being a ditz, and she barely knew me. Considering all that, telling her seems downright stupid. She got the information out of me, though, because I was sick of lying, and she asked point blank about my eyebrows. I considered the blender response or the blank look, but I just couldn't do it. I couldn't keep pretending not to hear the question.

So I told her the truth. I told her I had pulled out all the hair from my eyebrows and that I couldn't stop myself. Being honest was terrifying, but something had to give and I decided it was me. In hindsight, I wish I had told anyone *but* her. The reaction my words received wasn't pretty. She scrunched up her face in revulsion and said what I dreaded most, "Gross!" I doubted it could get any worse. She wasn't finished though.

I shriveled up inside and only felt smaller when I heard her advice: "Well, *stop*." For the record, stopping cold turkey sounded excellent to me. The only problem was that pulling was an addiction I had constant access to indulging. I doubt anyone would put an alcoholic in a room full of bourbon, whiskey, and wine, and casually tell them to just kick the habit.

I decided I didn't want to tell anyone my secret ever

again. However, my newfound resolution, like so many of my other intentions, didn't last, and I found myself bottling my secret in until I cracked. Roughly two months after my unfortunate confession, I had a breakdown. Not quite a meltdown of Britney Spears' proportions, but pretty bad nonetheless.

I was out of control with the pulling, miserable on speech and debate, and feeling very alone in the world. I barely had eyebrows, and my eyelashes were equally sparse. My mom nervously asked me what happened to my eyebrows, and the next thing I knew, I was bawling. My tears were uncontrollable, and I was inconsolable. My body quaked with tremors, and I felt like I was back outside Fred Meyer's, terrified I was about to be raped. The world was spinning beyond my control, and all I could do was let the tears move their way past my nonexistent eyelashes and down my face. I didn't want to pull, but I couldn't stop, and the whole thing made me feel inhuman. Instead I felt like some insect, and instead of biting off my mate's head after mating, I was the type of bug that ripped out my own hair. I was the praying mantis of humans. This sentiment gushed out of me with the tears, while my mom listened and stroked my hair. It felt so good to be touched there, but I was terrified she would be repulsed too. I couldn't bear to see my mom revolted like the girl from speech and debate.

I should have realized that it would take a lot more than hair removal to separate my mom from my side. She pulled me onto her lap and hugged me tightly as my story spilled out. It took several hours before I was calm enough to keep my words from getting garbled, which was when my mom decided it was time to know what we were up against with my pulling. She did what I had been too scared to do before—type the words "hair pulling" into the Google search bar. I think I was afraid that articles would appear showing the link between pulling and insanity. That was something I wasn't willing to face. My mom, however, thought it was time we got some answers.

She sat me down next to the computer and clicked on the first official-looking website, which was where I found out the name of the thing that had been torturing me for years: *trichotillomania* (commonly referred to as "trich"). Before that day, I didn't know there *was* an official name for my pulling, let alone so many addicts like me out there. On some level, I knew I wasn't totally alone, but at Ashland High School it sure felt that way.

The website we discovered changed everything for me. I found out there was an estimated one to two million people with trich in America alone. The reason for the broad range was because people like me were really good at hiding it. The website didn't say I was insane. It told me the urge felt irresistible and that all things considered, my case wasn't all that bad. It pointed out that some people continue pulling even when they are asleep. I also knew that not everyone was lucky enough to have a supportive mom and the resources to pay for therapy. That was a lot more than plenty of people could say.

Understanding that what I had was real and not a sign of insanity made a huge difference in my life. I could trust myself again. I stopped talking about "that crazy girl" when I was referring to myself in my head. It took a while, but eventually I stopped picturing myself as a praying mantis too. Knowing that what I had was real, somewhat common, and even had a name helped me come to terms with my addiction. I didn't need to feel ashamed I had a compulsive urge because lots of people have compulsive behaviors. It started to occur to me that maybe I was part of a silent majority—people who suffer from something but are too scared to talk about it with anyone. More importantly, after finding out about trich, I felt like I could talk to Gwyn about my pulling.

I was still scared to confide in her. My mom was obligated to love me no matter what, and Gwyn wasn't. Still, I thought if there was anyone my age I could count on for support, it was Gwyn. I couldn't stop obsessing about her reaction, though, and I planned out the perfect way to tell her everything.

It began with a walk around the Southern Oregon University campus, which was conveniently located near our houses. The evening was beautiful, cold, and crisp, and it felt good to stretch my legs while we walked familiar streets we had crossed together since elementary school. It took me a while to get around to the real reason I had asked her to go on the walk. She knew there was something I had to say, since usually when we were together we stayed in her house and sang (very badly) to whatever her iPod randomly selected. She waited patiently for me to spit it out and continued to listen until the whole story was dangling in the brisk air. Gwyn never so much as flinched. She just nodded her head at appropriate moments and asked me a series of questions. Gwyn asked me about the extent of my pulling, whether I needed any medical treatment for it, and whether I ate my hair. Her questions were important, and she asked them calmly, almost clinically, in the matter-of-fact way that had always been Gwyn's style.

Once she was satisfied my health wasn't in any serious danger and she didn't need her parents (both of whom were doctors) to take me to the hospital, she told me my condition didn't matter to her. I had been her friend when I couldn't tie my own shoes and had traded my Fruit Roll-up for her fruit leathers. We had been friends when I was the geekiest, dorkiest girl at Lincoln Elementary School, couldn't climb the rope ladder, and read books during lunch. My pulling was meaningless compared to all that. We would be friends even if I was completely bald. Gwyn's confident smile reminded me that at the end of the day, friends are there to have your back, even when some of your family fails to support you.

My dad and I had gotten into a pattern where everything was quid pro quo. "I'll take you to a museum, honey—if you fly down to see me exclusively." Great. Trich was no different to him; it was just another thing to haggle over. My mom wanted me in therapy. She thought it was best if I got as much help as possible to beat my addiction. I think it was hard for her to see firsthand what I was doing to myself too. Whenever I was stressed or sleep-deprived, the pulling became worse, and I would lose huge chunks of eyebrow in the space of a few hours. My mom wanted me to see a professional psychologist as soon as possible.

But, therapy meant I had to get my dad to pay half the bill, something he typically resisted. He had only helped pay for therapy before because he thought Carrie the Therapist would pressure me into speaking to him more often. Still, I figured he would find my trich so disturbing that he would cover half of therapy. Of course, it was never that simple with my dad.

It's a rare individual who can use his daughter's disorder to make life even *more* miserable for her, but my dad could do it without qualms or apologies. He refused to supply a dime if there were changes I could make at home to solve my "problem." His first recommendation was to get rid of our dogs. He decided (being such an expert on trich and all . . . *not!*) that there was a link between my pets and my pulling. According to my father, our two dogs were creating stress in my life.

My dad had other suggestions too, most of which involved medication. I was not interested in pursuing this path. I could feel pretty crummy sometimes (just like everyone else), but that didn't stop me from being an upbeat, optimistic person. I got a rush of happiness from rollerblading, goofing around with my friends, and watching cheesy romantic comedies, among other things. I didn't want to lose any of that because of medications. I was haunted by a Cheryl Wheeler song that questions whether people can really tell the difference between feeling peace and Prozac. I didn't want to feel nothing at all—I'd already experienced living numb in middle school. That had been enough to steer me away from medication, although I have heard for some people it can be helpful. I didn't need Tom Cruise spouting

Scientology to know that drugs just weren't the best option for me. In fact, my mom rolled her eyes when I told her my dad's suggestion and replied, "You don't need that." It took awhile for my dad to realize there was no way I would get rid of the pets, put myself on drugs, or trade in my home for some type of rehab facility. After a lot of begging, pleading, and pulling, he agreed to help pay for my therapy. That was where I began working out my pulling issues and a drug-free existence was recommended to me. I just wish everyone in my family had been able to stay clean.

Chapter I7

MY COUSIN AUSTIN HAD always been one of the most important people in my life. As kids, we were inseparable troublemakers who thrived on stirring up problems with our shenanigans. Austin and I had a lot in common: we were both friendly, extroverted, vaguely mischievous, and intelligent. Growing up, I secretly thought we were the same person. I imagined us as a penny—we were different on just the matter of our genders, but inside we were made of the same metal. Maybe that's why I turned to pulling while he turned to drugs.

I had never understood drugs, which is why I did the extra credit rape project in high school. When I heard the term "uppers" and "downers," I stared in confusion, before asking why anyone would want to get depressed on drugs. As far as

I was concerned, drugs were what the "bad" kids did in their free time. None of my friends had expressed an interest in experimenting with altered states of consciousness, so I chose to pretend that drugs just didn't exist. When Austin became an addict, I had to reevaluate everything.

Austin wasn't just some random druggie; he was my on-again, off-again role model. While I was walking the straight and narrow, he was partying and socializing and being "cool." I had accepted my status as Queen of the Nerds with much pleasure, but I still longed for a bit of excitement. I wanted to see the world through Austin's eyes. At least I did, until that involved cocaine and heroin. Hearing reports from my grandma about how Austin was having run-ins with the police, how he was getting into trouble at his wretched private high school, how he was slipping up and getting himself hurt scared me. I just didn't know what I could do stuck in Ashland while he battled his demons in Manhattan Beach, California.

The summer before my senior year of high school, I flew down to Los Angeles to stay at my grandma's just as Austin hit rock bottom. He had been busted for drug possession again and needed to go to rehab or juvenile hall. Grandma was absolutely frantic. She had always felt the need to fix everyone's problems and was working double-time to extract

Austin from the mess he'd made of his life. Grandma kept making arrangements and whispering secretively into the cell phone the whole time I was in Los Angeles. I knew I was only underfoot and that the way I could be most helpful was to ensure that I wasn't in the way.

I escaped to the closest Barnes & Noble every day to get my mind off the Austin situation. I still felt tense and worried, but I was able to submerge my fears in books. Morally, I did have a few pangs about my behavior. I knew it was wrong to go into a bookstore, spend all day reading, and leave without making a single purchase. On the other hand, I never could have afforded to buy all those books. So, I did my best to blend into the background and even hid under a desk in order to inconspicuously enjoy everything the YA fiction section had to offer.

My visit with Grandma, however, wasn't the relaxing stay I had originally imagined. Instead, I couldn't wait to fly out to Atlanta and join the group of Jewish teenagers from all over the United States who would be traveling across the country on a bus with me. That was my *real* summer plan.

The program was called Etgar 36, and it promised I would feel an increased sense of connection with my country while I met with people involved in solving important issues (like homelessness, gun control, immigration, and abortion). I was excited about the trip, but mainly I was looking forward to leaving Los Angeles. It was killing me to be in the same state, the same freaking city, as my cousin, and still be unable to help him pull his life together. I thought going away on Etgar would help clear my head.

I was partly right. Etgar was an amazing experience that completely surpassed everything they advertised on the website. We did so many things in the course of a day—meetings, museums, historical landmarks, national monuments—it was insane in the best possible way. It was hard to find the energy to obsess over my cousin when I was always on the move and surrounded by interesting teenagers. Even the quiet time I spent on the bus staring out the window as states rolled by me was spent in peaceful thought. Instead of the mountains I was used to seeing, there were stretches where my view went uninterrupted. I would soak in the sights and wonder what it would be like to walk off into a horizon that seemed to stretch to eternity.

The group of us boarded the bus in Atlanta and made our way back across the country to Los Angeles before splitting into two camps: a group of kids who would fly to Chicago and continue onward (I was in this group) and the kids who would head back home. I had mixed feelings about returning to the city I had just left, even though it was only for a day. All my anxiety over Austin came bubbling up to the surface, especially when I heard we were scheduled to go to a Jewish rehab center for dinner. I didn't know who I could confide in about my fears for Austin. I had made a bunch of friends on the cross-country trip, but I didn't think Austin's drug use was my secret to tell. I wanted to protect him as much as possible, so I kept my mouth shut.

The rehab center sent all my tightly-bottled control spattering everywhere. Just walking in the front doors scared me. I knew any minute my fears about Austin were going to smother me. The truth was, I was terrified that Austin, the cousin I had played hide-and-go-seek with, was going to disappear. I would be left looking at an empty shell. I was afraid that even though we had been best friends, distance and time had made it impossible for me to reach him. I'd always felt out of control with my trich, but Austin's problem was absolutely beyond me alone—that was what made panic rise. There was nothing I could do to help him.

The drug addicts sat in a circle with our group and told their stories. They explained how they had gotten hooked on various substances and how their addictions had taken over their lives. They said that what they cared about the most, what they needed the most, was getting their fix. I pictured Austin the whole time, imagined the words coming from his mouth, and the desperation kept swelling. We weren't even eighteen years old. Pulling and rehab weren't supposed to happen to Austin and me. The addicts sharing their life stories weren't supposed to become us.

I had a mini-epiphany while we heard about one man's experience with heroin—addiction isn't just for the "bad" kids. All my life, I had been thinking about addiction like a stupid anti-drug poster. "Just say no." It's not that easy. I had avoided drugs and alcohol, I had taken all the AP classes, I had steered clear from video games, I had immersed myself in books from a young age. And at the end of all that, I was still trapped under the weight of addiction.

Something clicked in my brain at that rehab center, and I realized I'd been right about Austin all along. We were the same person. We both turned to something that made us feel good, that helped us escape from our minds and the world. The only real difference was that his addiction was illegal and had landed him in rehab, whereas my addiction was misunderstood and socially stigmatizing. The stereotype of the "good kid" I had always tried to fill and the "bad kid" that Austin's private school was trying to make him out to be, appeared to me then as nothing more than a pile of *merde*. He was my cousin, my flip side, and, as far as I was concerned, there was no one better.

I called my mom that night and told her how worried I was about him. I asked her just how badly Austin was doing and choked back tears when I heard her answer. My mom told me to let the family worry about Austin and enjoy myself on the trip. She pointed out what I already knew—it was out of my hands. All of this happened while the group was chowing down on pizza. I spent the dinner with my cell phone to my ear, trying not to bawl. My mom suggested I talk to an addict at the rehab if I thought it would make me feel better. I decided it was better than doing nothing, so I asked our first speaker if there was any way I could make things easier for Austin. The man just shook his head and told me straight up that, "All you can do is be supportive."

I wanted to see Austin, or even just talk to him on the phone, and tell him again that I was sure he could kick the habit. I've always had faith in Austin. Maybe that's a little strange considering the state he was in, but I still believed he could beat the drugs and alcohol. If there was anyone who had the inner strength to chase demons away, it was Austin. But I couldn't talk to him. Austin was at his rehab center, so I had to be content with passing the message through my mom to my grandma to him.

It was time for my group to fly to Chicago, and I didn't want to go. My family was in turmoil and while only a few weeks ago I couldn't wait to leave, now all I wanted was to stay put. Austin, my grandma, and my mom were all on the West Coast. That was where I thought I should be too. I had enjoyed the Etgar experience, and three weeks on a bus had been a wonderful adventure, but I was ready to see it draw to a close.

I had signed up for the full Etgar package, though, which meant waving good-bye to my closest friends in Los Angeles and continuing on to Chicago. I felt strange touching down in the Windy City. I had always wanted to see it, and now my enthusiasm seemed all dried up. Maybe it was the jet lag, but I decided it would be best if I stayed to myself. There were still a bunch of great kids in the group, but things had become a bit cliquish, and my closest friends had exited stage left in California. With only ten more days to go, I was prepared to spend my time with just my thoughts and music for company. Luckily, I never had to take such drastic measures.

There was one late arrival joining us in Chicago. It was a girl who had gone on the first half of the trip the year before and was planning to finish the second half with us. I don't think anyone really cared. We were all too preoccupied with our own lives to think much about the new girl. It's possible that if she hadn't been one of my roommates that first night we wouldn't have bonded. Not that I was excited about having my room of three girls become a room of four. What I really wanted was my king-sized bed I had left behind in Ashland. Still, I knew I was already cohabitating with a confirmed narcissist who hijacked the bathroom every morning. What was one more undesirable roommate?

I didn't make a particularly good first impression on the new girl. I was frustrated with my other roommate and irked with myself for feeling so gloomy. So, I did what any irrational teenage girl would do. I grabbed my iPod and started dancing in the closet. Blasting the soundtrack from *Dirty Dancing: Havana Nights* did have a soothing effect, and I finally emerged ready to meet the roommate. Enter Stephanie.

Stephanie was completely unlike anyone I had ever met before. After introducing herself, she felt the need to say, "I'm horny." This led to a moment of more than a little awkwardness. I quickly learned that Stephanie was virtually incapable of censoring herself. She said what she thought without wasting time trying to be tactful. I actually found it refreshing. Her candor was part of her charm. I also thought she was a little insane. Who makes out with a boy on a summer trip the first night and proceeds to discuss the indiscretion, in detail, with her boyfriend over the phone? Stephanie.

The crazy thing is, we meshed instantly and became really

good friends. Stephanie helped me find my misplaced enthusiasm and together we made an unbeatable team. I had a buddy again, someone to keep an eye out for me and vice versa. We swapped music, shared a room, went shopping, and were generally inseparable. She never stopped surprising me. I confided in her about the time I slobbered all over Graham and in return she told me about the time she dated an Orthodox Jew whose father hadn't approved. (The fact that they were caught making out in front of the Torah might not have helped.)

Stephanie kept me laughing and made me try new things. She was the one who took me (clueless as ever) to my first sex store. It was a complete accident. I hadn't seen the name of the store—I just noticed some of our friends inside and agreed to check it out. I noticed the door handles shaped in the letters CK, which I thought stood for Calvin Klein or something. They didn't. They actually stood for Condom Kingdom. Inside was the largest display of unmentionables imaginable. I got super embarrassed, but the other girls just seemed curious. Aaron, the only boy in the group, shifted nervously like we might inquire about the size of his anatomy, while Stephanie pointed out various objects in her possession or that her boyfriend was about to get for her. That was a little too much information for me. We left without making a purchase but with a new appreciation for the male physique.

It took me a while to completely open up to Stephanie. We were close enough for me to really care about her opinion of me, and I didn't want to creep her out with my trich. I almost didn't say anything, but much to my surprise the topic came up while riding on the bus from Washington, D.C. to North Carolina. It started with me telling her about my dad's attempt at amends by sending me possums in a nutshell—a hand-painted walnut that opened to reveal a picnic scene of possums. He told me that any woman would want it and certainly any fourteen-year-old girl, because who doesn't love a good possum in a walnut? Stephanie and I were talking about parents and life when I realized she deserved to know about the pulling. We had braved horrible roommates, dingy motels, cockroaches, and mobs of people scrambling to buy the last Harry Potter book. I knew her secrets—it was only fair that she knew mine.

I was nervous about telling Stephanie about trich. I had barely gotten to the word "pulling" when she asked me if I had trich. I was shocked. I had no idea how she could have figured it out so quickly. Had she seen any hairless patches and suspected my secret? The answer to that was, surprisingly—no. Stephanie knew I meant trich because she had trich. She didn't need me to explain because she dealt with the same problem every day. For the first time, I had found someone I knew who understood precisely what I was talking about.

There are a lot of fears that go along with trich that you don't really have until you start pulling. That's part of what made me feel so alone—not knowing anyone who had the same anxieties as I did. I didn't know anyone else who was afraid of getting haircuts, not because they might be trimmed too close, but because the people in the shop would stare at your head in horror and ask what had happened. I was terrified of getting lice on Etgar (there was an outbreak, but it was cleared up pretty fast), not because I feared the little buggers but because I didn't want anyone looking closely at my scalp. I had once loved windy days, but with trich those no longer held any enjoyment. Walking to school knowing that a gust of air could expose me to ridicule and censure forced me to constantly hold my bangs down. This made me look odd in itself. There are also the fears of a teacher requiring you to take off a hat, someone wanting to put your hair into a French braid, going into a swimming pool where individual hairs cling together and reveal the pulling even to the untrained eye. All of these things don't usually occur to people who don't suffer from trich. It was wonderful to talk to someone who knew exactly what I was up against.

The two of us didn't close our mouths once until we had reached the hotel hours later. There was so much to share. That had been the one secret between us, and with that wall down, we could ask anything without fear. She asked me if there had been any signs growing up that I had trich. Apparently, she had pulled out all the hair from her stuffed animals as a child. Stephanie had also had a rougher time getting support from her parents. They tried to frighten her into a pull-free life and succeeded only in scaring her.

We shared our pasts and I felt less . . . haunted. Trich had always been my solitary burden, up to me alone to feel, and now it was different. I wasn't alone. Trich and life in general might have been working to make me feel helpless and lonely, but it couldn't succeed with Stephanie by my side. I had proof that it wasn't just me. When Stephanie told me she had trich, suddenly those millions of other people with trich weren't just part of a statistic on a website. Stephanie and I had found each other and that gave me a lot of hope. Maybe, I wouldn't feel the need to hide my flaw, my addiction, forever. Surrounded by people like Stephanie, Gwyn, and my mom, maybe I could someday be able to love myself and admit I had trich at the same time. I felt like I could let the world know who Marni really is without fear.

Epilogue

JUST IN CASE YOU'RE WONDERING . . . I did get into college. I'm currently a student at Lewis & Clark College in Oregon where I *still* have had no romantic success with boys. I still embarrass myself on a regular basis, but I take it in stride. At least there is no shortage of amusement, and, quite frankly, I wouldn't want my life any other way.

I still pull. I wish I could say that college has shown me the error of my ways, but that just isn't true. I pull because it feels so good, it is still too hard to quit. Since I've been in college, I have become better at keeping my pulling in check. I think this is because I am happier in college than I ever was in high school. Maybe it isn't the Neverland I originally imagined, but it has its magical moments. As far as the pulling goes, all I can do is try my hardest and take it one day at a time. I remain optimistic that someday I'll be able to kick the habit entirely.

I still talk to Stephanie, and she gives me updates about the craziness in her life. College has done nothing to dilute my amazement at her tenacity. She also continues to pull but flat-out refuses to let it control her life. While Stephanie and I still struggle with trich, Austin has done an amazing job of turning his life around. He got out of rehab, took a long look at himself, and started making changes. Now he is in college, proving everyone who ever doubted him wrong. The two of us have been able to relate because of our addictions in a way I never imagined possible. If there is a silver lining to having trich, it is the way it has brought me closer to Austin.

Shayna is doing great. She is graduating from college this year and is ready to meet the challenges of the so-called real world. We've grown closer over the years, and we can now talk on the phone about the latest episodes of our favorite shows. Hopefully, someday things will be even better, but for now, I'm happy with our relationship.

I still have trouble deciphering my dad. Recently, the two of us saw each other for the first time in five years. He took me shopping, spent an exorbitant amount of money, and left—our relationship just as fuzzy and unclear as before. I pretty much haven't heard from him since. I have no great expectations on this front. Seemingly he contacts me when it serves his purposes.

In hindsight, high school doesn't seem quite so dreadful. I still remember hating it and longing to leave, but it turns out I wasn't as invisible as I thought. In fact, I was nominated for a bunch of Senior "Most Likelys" (and won Forever Sober, which I am still trying to disprove). I keep in touch with my high school friends, including Gwyn, and relish having conversations with them that don't include SAT scores and upcoming AP tests. That's another refreshing thing I found out about college: test scores don't really matter. Once you are in, you're in. After that, all that matters is what you do with yourself.

So what's next? Three years of college and countless essays from now I'll probably be an English major and doing . . . something. What did you expect? I don't know where my life is going. I'm absolutely clueless about my real ending. Hopefully, this book will go on to critical acclaim, change lives, and score me an invitation to talk to Jon Stewart on *The Daily Show* (or Oprah). If not, well, I intend to keep writing and hope I can support myself by doing what I love. I still panic at the thought of joining the working class and intend to take advantage of college while it lasts.

Anyhow, that's me. Or at least me right now. Let's face it—I'm going to change a lot between now and . . . forty. This only encapsulates my first nineteen years of life and hopefully has made you feel a little less alone in the world. That's what writing it has done for me. Sure it was frightening to write about my life and put it out into the world for friends, acquaintances, and strangers to see. In fact, when I first started writing, it felt like I was dragging myself out of the closet. After hiding this huge part of myself all through high school, the idea of revealing it in college terrified me.

I wanted to make a new start at Lewis & Clark, and telling the world about my problems didn't seem like the best way to do that. I instantly began to fear social rejection and outcast status. I couldn't exactly look to any notable figures to explain the disorder to my friends either, since there is no Ellen DeGeneres of trich. It made me nervous at first to be discussing something so private that is never discussed. It scared me so much, I had to see the school therapist for advice.

But then this really amazing thing happened: by being candid and honest, other people started telling me their own stories. It seems that, not only does everyone have their own inner demons—they also know someone else who is battling an addiction. I've met other kids with trich because of this book, and the more I discuss what I've been through, the more comfortable with myself I've become. I've gotten more out of this book than all my therapy sessions because I'm not only helping myself. I'm doing this to help others. And if that works, if you feel like you have more compassion and understanding for people with compulsive behaviors, then this book and my life have been a success. I think that would be the nicest possible outcome.

As a kid, I turned to books for help, and now (hopefully) I've written a book that other kids can turn to. That seems fitting to me. But what do I know? I'm just Marni.

Best of luck,
Marni Bates

Book Club Discussion Questions for MARNI

1. Prior to reading *MARNI*, had you heard of trichotillomania? What did you learn about this stress disorder? Its causes? Its symptoms?

2. Despite the fact that the author struggles with a difficult family dynamic and challenging stress disorder, much of her writing has a light and often humorous tone. How does the writing style of *MARNI* work for the subject matter she is writing about?

3. Marni writes about the lack of discussion on pulling in her high school health classes. What stress-related and emotional disorders do you see among your peers? How are they different from trich? What are the similarities? Is information on these disorders readily available?

4. Much of *MARNI* is devoted to the dysfunctional relationship the author has with her estranged dad. In what ways do you think this relationship may have played a role in the author developing trich?

5. In *MARNI*, we follow the author's journey from a precocious elementary student to high school senior. What do you think Marni's biggest challenge or issue was at the

beginning of the book? Did she resolve this issue by the end of the book? Why or why not?

6. Have you ever felt like you had a personal secret that was too embarrassing to share with anyone else? Did you end up letting anyone in on what was happening or keep it buried within yourself? How did your choice make you feel? Does it still affect you today?

7. Students with disorders like binging and cutting can often hide their habits from the rest of the world. But Marni was always in fear of being discovered—someone might notice her nonexistent eyebrows or the pile of hair she left behind after a pulling session in class. How would it feel to go through high school living in fear of having your darkest, deepest secret discovered? How might this impact your self-esteem? Your body image? Your social life?

8. Did you relate to the author and her experiences? If so, in what ways?

9. Did Marni have any "a ha" moments where she made an important discovery about herself which allowed to her grow? What were these moments? What did she learn in each one?

About the Author

Marni Bates is a freshman at Lewis & Clark College. She wrote her first novel, *That's Debatable*, between filling out college applications and is currently looking for an agent. She loves writing and hopes to do it professionally throughout her life. Marni was recommended for this series by the The Oregon Writing Project at Willamette University.